When the Enemy Strikes

Also by Charles F. Stanley
in Large Print:

Winning the War Within
Seeking His Face: A Daily Devotional
Walking Wisely: Real Guidance
   for Life's Journey
The Blessings of Brokenness:
   Why God Allows Us to Go Through
   Hard Times

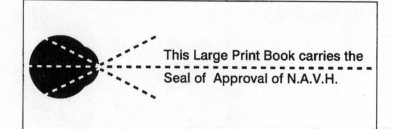

This Large Print Book carries the
Seal of Approval of N.A.V.H.

When the Enemy Strikes

The Keys to Winning Your
Spiritual Battles

Charles F. Stanley

Thorndike Press • Waterville, Maine

Published in 2005 by arrangement with Thomas Nelson, Inc.

Thorndike Press® Large Print Inspirational.

The tree indicium is a trademark of Thorndike Press.

The text of this Large Print edition is unabridged.
Other aspects of the book may vary from the original edition.

Set in 16 pt. Plantin by Carleen Stearns.

Printed in the United States on permanent paper.

Library of Congress Cataloging-in-Publication Data

Stanley, Charles F.
    When the enemy strikes : the keys to winning your
spiritual battles / by Charles F. Stanley. — Large print ed.
        p. cm.
    ISBN 0-7862-8078-6 (lg. print : hc : alk. paper)
    1. Spiritual warfare.   2. Large type books.   I. Title.
BV4509.5.S825 2005
235′.4—dc22   2005019824

To Gearl Spicer,
devoted servant of God and administrative
pastor at First Baptist Church of Atlanta.
We have "fought the good fight" side-by-
side many times. My friend, I am deeply
grateful.

As the Founder/CEO of NAVH, the only national health agency solely devoted to those who, although not totally blind, have an eye disease which could lead to serious visual impairment, I am pleased to recognize Thorndike Press* as one of the leading publishers in the large print field.

Founded in 1954 in San Francisco to prepare large print textbooks for partially seeing children, NAVH became the pioneer and standard setting agency in the preparation of large type.

Today, those publishers who meet our standards carry the prestigious "Seal of Approval" indicating high quality large print. We are delighted that Thorndike Press is one of the publishers whose titles meet these standards. We are also pleased to recognize the significant contribution Thorndike Press is making in this important and growing field.

Lorraine H. Marchi, L.H.D.
Founder/CEO
NAVH

* Thorndike Press encompasses the following imprints: Thorndike, Wheeler, Walker and Large Print Press.

Contents

1

The Face of Evil

I still vividly remember how I felt on December 7, 1941. It was on that fateful Sunday afternoon as a boy of nine that I first heard about the Japanese surprise attack at Pearl Harbor. I watched as our small town of Danville, Virginia, began to deal with the possibilities of a war. An unexpected enemy had struck, and our lives would never be the same.

Likewise, no one would have predicted the terrorist attacks on our nation September 11, 2001. When those airplanes were crashed into the World Trade Center and the Pentagon, our fast-paced society came to a sudden stop. The unthinkable had occurred. America had been assaulted by a foe that hated us because of who we are and what we believe.

Throughout our lives we face many different types of enemies. Some are motivated by personal reasons. A person may dislike you for any number of reasons — he may be jealous of your success or perhaps want to take from you something he desires for himself. Once in awhile you may be hated so much that someone might want to harm you in a very serious way or even end your life.

When you know your foe and are prepared for the attack, victory is achievable. But I have found that the greatest enemies are unknown and unexpected. For instance, a trusted friend who turns against you when she sees the potential for personal gain. A coworker who gossips and schemes against you in hopes of a promotion. Or a thief hiding in the night waiting to rob you. The motivation that all these enemies share in common is found in the root of evil.

Evil. It is something we know exists, but it is not a topic we like to think about or confront. Evil has a face. It is dangerous . . . dark . . . foreboding . . . deadly. Do you know what is the ultimate source of evil? Are you aware of how evil operates? If you don't know how it works, then how can you adequately protect yourself and your loved ones against its sudden attack?

Sorting Out Good and Evil

We all know that both good and evil exist in our world. We are taught from early childhood that some things are bad, and some are good. We are taught as children that we need to develop an ability to distinguish between good and evil. As we grow up, we are cautioned to be alert to circumstances around us so we might avoid evil and choose to associate with what is good.

But when I ask individuals if they have a difficult time discerning good from evil, they often reply, "Yes, I do. There's a lot of 'gray' in the world today."

Most seem to agree about certain types of evil. It's wrong for a parent to abandon a child or to abuse a child physically, sexually, or emotionally. It's wrong for suicide bombers to blow up innocent people. It's wrong for a person to kill another person in cold blood or to torture another person.

There are a host of things that are immediately and universally labeled as wrong — demonstrating racial prejudice, having blind hatred for someone, embezzling or mismanaging corporate funds, cheating on a test, lying, failing to help a person in need when you have means to help, stealing, committing adultery, exhibiting road rage, engaging in a drive-by shooting, kidnapping, raping, drinking to excess, using illegal drugs, and carrying out many other bad behaviors and holding on to wrong-thinking attitudes.

We can look at certain situations and recognize an aspect of evil embedded in them — for example, a wasting, painful disease; suffering of all kinds; world hunger; abject poverty; intense persecution of good people; or deep agony over the loss of a child. We may not be able to pinpoint the exact nature or cause of the evil, but we sense that the bad situation has an element of darkness to it. We recognize that things are not as they should be in a perfect world.

We are quick to label all of these actions, attitudes, and conditions as being marked indelibly by evil. But then comes the difficult question: "Is the person who committed this evil act or holds a wrong attitude an evil person?"

"Well, now," people say as they back-pedal into justification, "the person is probably good deep down inside. He didn't really mean to do what he did — he's just a product of his upbringing, his culture, or his fanatical religion. He just got blinded temporarily by greed or lust. The person didn't know what he was doing — he was temporarily insane."

We often conclude, "People are good, but their behaviors are bad." We may even say, "We love and hold out hope for the sinner, but the sin is bad."

All of that may be true, but what do you do when evil strikes you?

What do you say and how do you respond when you are the victim of spousal abuse, the object of a terrorist's actions, or the one badly injured by a drunk driver?

What do you do when your loved one is held hostage, your child is abused by an adult you and your child trusted, you come home to find your home burglarized, or you receive the diagnosis of a terminal disease?

How do you discern good from evil when you are the one who is the victim of an evil attack?

What do you do when you recognize that you don't always act in a positive, godly, or wise way toward other people? What happens when the mirror of stark reality is held up before your face and you are forced to admit, "I'm the one who is inflicting pain; I'm the one who is lashing out with an evil intent or a wrong attitude"?

How do you deal with issues of good and evil when you see them at work, and at war, within you?

Recognizing evil, dealing with it, seeking to pursue good and avoid evil, acknowledging evil in ourselves and turning it to good — these issues are at the core of our human existence. If we truly could be objective about our lives, we would probably find that we spend the majority of any given day trying to do the things that we label as good and right, and avoiding situations, relationships, encounters, and circumstances that we label as bad or wrong.

At times, we fail miserably at both — we don't do what we know is right, and we do what we know is wrong.

How do we keep our balance? How do we effectively pursue good and turn from evil? What do we do when we suddenly seem to be the victims of evil?

These questions are at the heart of this book.

The answers are rooted in God's Word.

The Bible clearly teaches two things about evil:

1. *You have a powerful enemy, and he has a name.* For years some people have talked about God in general terms. He's

their Higher Power, the Force, or the Man Upstairs. The truth is, good has a name, and His name is God.

Evil also has a name. His name is Satan or the devil. The devil refers to a spiritual being who is the supreme personification of evil. Lucifer is the Bible name for one of God's archangels who rebelled against God and was cast to the earth where he functions as Satan or the devil. (In this book, we'll use the terms *Satan* and *the devil* interchangeably.) He seeks to rule from the realm of the unseen — the spiritual dimension.

Satan may use what your mother-in-law says or a coworker does to come against you. He may use terrorists, criminals, and other people to cause you harm or strike fear into your heart. However, the person who verbally abuses you, the thief who robs you, the critic who maligns you, the rival who undercuts or thwarts your good efforts, or the assailant who beats you is not your real enemy. The real enemy is the devil who prompted the person to speak hatred to you, steal from you, do his utmost to destroy you or physically injure you.

Behind every evil person and every evil act lurks the real enemy of your life. He exists in the spirit realm, and he is relentless in his pursuit of you. He is 100 percent evil, and he has a plan to destroy your life.

Satan is your enemy.

2. *You are in a spiritual battle.* It doesn't matter whether you want to be in a spiritual battle — you are in one. The battle is between good and evil, and you are the prize. God desires to have a relationship with you, bless you, and live with you forever. Satan desires to keep you from all that God wants for you. He is the enemy of all people — followers of Jesus or not. He is your enemy!

You are a prime target of the devil. He will do his utmost to keep you from the truth that Jesus is your Savior, and through Him you can receive forgiveness and the gift of eternal life. Satan will attempt to entrap you in any way he can to keep you from God. His target is your eternal spirit.

"I'm a Christian," you may say. "I already belong to God. The devil can't have my spirit."

If you have made a commitment to Jesus as your Savior and Lord, you are absolutely correct in saying that your spirit already belongs to God and the devil can lay no claim on your eternal destiny. The sa-

16

tanic forces can do other things to you, however.

He can and will attempt to drag you down into such deep bondage that you will lose your joy in living. Some may call this bondage oppression, depression, or addiction. If the devil can pull you into bondage, you will have no peace, no zest for living, and perhaps even no will to continue living. You will struggle continually with desires that are not met, drives that are not satisfied, dreams that are not realized, and a destiny that is unfulfilled. The devil will do his utmost to completely destroy anything that is essential for abundant life.

The devil can and will work against you to keep you from having any positive witness for Jesus Christ in this world. He will do his utmost to steal from you the resources you might use to extend the gospel, destroy your reputation so that anything you say about the Lord is suspect, and kill your valuable relationships with other people so that you are demoralized and don't believe you can influence another person for Christ.

So how are we to deal with the devil? How can we combat our true enemy and resist his spiritual attacks?

The first rule of any battle is this: know

your enemy. If you don't know your enemy, how can you fight him? How can you stand and be victorious against an enemy you can't or haven't identified?

Yes, we must know the nature of our enemy. We must understand who he is and how he works.

2

The Nature of Our Enemy

I knew from the look on the nurse's face that something was wrong. As soon as she removed the bandages, she abruptly said, "I'll get the doctor." With that, she whirled around and hurried from the room. Her words were not unusual. The tone in which she spoke them and the look in her eyes were the real indicators that something was badly wrong.

For his part, the doctor seemed evasive. "These things take time. This can be normal. Nothing is ever entirely predictable."

The truth was, the surgery was not a complete success, and for my part, the results were not what I expected. It appeared to me that no amount of time was going to remedy the problem. The result was disfiguring and painful, and worst of all, my vision was affected. My eyes watered continually, and when my vision wasn't badly blurred, I had double vision. I was left unable to read, study, or do virtually anything that required the use of my eyes. And this went on week after week.

I was unable to do the reading and studying necessary to prepare sermons. I was out of the pulpit for several months. I was unable to drive, unable to take photographs or develop film in my darkroom, unable to watch videos or news programs, unable to focus visually for very long on visitors who came to see me.

I was physically miserable and, most of the time, bored for a lack of things to do.

My situation was very difficult, and it left me open to spiritual attack. My eyesight was in jeopardy, and my body was in pain. The more intense attacks of the enemy were to come in the middle of the night, at unexpected quiet moments, and many times, as I prayed.

The enemy whispered into my spirit, "You'll never see again. You'll never be able to read the Bible again for longer than just a few words or a couple of verses. You'll never be able to preach freely again."

If I didn't move quickly to squelch those lies, the enemy continued his taunts, "You're finished. It's over. You'll never do again what you love to do and have devoted your life to. The ministry has had its day."

Those whispers of the enemy were just as much a spiritual attack as the attack I was experiencing in my eyes. The battleground was in the spirit realm. The assaults of the enemy were on my mind and heart. And the real challenge I faced was not the challenge of recovering my eyesight and physical health. The real challenge was overcoming the attack of the enemy against my soul.

The same is true for every person.

The obvious external assault of the enemy on our lives — dealing us a blow in our bodies, in our finances, or in our relationships — is not the ultimate spiritual attack we face. The ultimate assault is aimed at the soul — mind, emotions, and will.

It is with the will that we choose whether to accept Jesus as our Savior. It is with the will that we choose to follow Jesus as Lord.

It is in our emotions that we are motivated to do our utmost for the Lord on this earth or to give up and give in to life's troubles.

It is in our minds that we develop the attitudes and beliefs that give rise to all we say and do.

The devil desires first and foremost your spirit. But if he cannot have your spirit, he will go after your soul. And very often he will inflict pain and hardship on your physical body or your external finances, possessions, and relationships in order to strike at your soul.

You must know with certainty these things about your enemy:

- Satan is real.
- He never gives up his pursuit of us.
- Satanic forces have a plan of attack.

The Devil Is Real

Some people say, "Oh, I don't believe in the devil."

Satan loves to hear that! The devil loves it when people refuse to believe in him. That means he is totally camouflaged and covered by their lack of belief. That means he can come in under the radar, totally undetected.

If a person doesn't believe in the devil, he'll never seek to understand the traps he continues to fall into. He'll never seek to understand how to conquer the negative, debilitating, addictive, downward spiral of temptation. He'll never understand how to keep from yielding to temptation. He'll never learn how to overcome guilt or deal with low self-worth, both of which weaken a person and make him even more susceptible to temptations and attacks.

The question is not whether the devil exists, whether we are engaged in spiritual warfare, or whether we are tempted. The answers are clear. The devil does exist, we are engaged in spiritual warfare, and we are tempted. The question we must ask is, "How can we survive the devil's attacks?"

First, we must recognize he has an army of evil helpers, spirits (demons) all committed to evil. Satan uses these minions to do his will to attempt to thwart God and His eternal purposes.

Every person who has ever done battle with one believes in demons. People who have been possessed by demons certainly believe in them. It is naïve to say, "I don't believe in a spiritual reality of darkness and evil." And it is especially double minded to say you don't believe in demons if you profess to believe in angels as ministers of love, joy, and peace to God's people.

Both good and evil are embodied in the spirit realm by very different entities — evil is embodied by demonic spirits. Now, that doesn't mean a demon is behind every bush or every bad event involves a specific demon. It does mean that spiritual forces of evil are behind every evil act. We need to remember always that our enemy — ultimately — is the devil and his demonic forces, not a human being who mistreats us in some way. The apostle Paul stated this very clearly: "We do not wrestle against flesh and blood" (Eph. 6:12).

The Bible tells us several specific things about the nature of our enemy.

The Devil Is Invisible

Satan doesn't look like a terrible monster or dark cloud and tempt you or make you angry. In fact, he does what he can to disguise himself and make himself invisible so he won't be blamed or fought as the enemy. He'll manipulate circumstances and situations against you. He will use people against you — people who will abuse you, misuse you, and confuse you!

The Devil Is Organized

We are arrayed against a vast host of evil. We are in a battle against "principalities, against powers, against the rulers of the darkness of this age, against spiritual hosts of wickedness in the heavenly places" (Eph. 6:12).

The Devil Is a Murderer, a Liar, and a Thief

Jesus described the devil in these ways: "He was a murderer from the beginning, and does not stand in the truth, because there is no truth in him. When he speaks a lie, he speaks from his own resources, for he is a liar and the father of it" (John 8:44).

Jesus also said, "The thief does not come except to steal, and to kill, and to destroy" (John 10:10).

The Devil Is Crafty and Scheming

The apostle Paul wrote to the Corinthians: "I fear, lest somehow, as the serpent deceived Eve by his craftiness, so your minds may be corrupted from the simplicity that is in Christ" (2 Cor. 11:3). Note three key words in this one verse:

1. Deceived. The devil attempts to deceive us by convincing us that right is wrong and wrong is right. To be deceived is to believe a lie. The devil has absolutely no capacity to tell the full truth about anything.

2. Craftiness. This word refers to shrewdness in manipulation — clever tricks, schemes, and strategies. The devil doesn't come at us head-on. He finds a back door, a missing link, or a point of weakness. He preys upon what we believe has been dealt with. He specializes in those things about which we are in denial. The devil does his utmost to conceal his identity and disguise himself as he deals with us.

3. Corrupted. This word has been translated in some versions as "seduced." The word in the original Greek means to be led astray subtly, but nonetheless brought off course from a pure devotion to Christ Jesus. The person who is corrupted or seduced by a temptation follows the passions and desires of his own self rather than the will and commands of God.

The devil strikes very shrewdly at our weaknesses. He comes at us at the point where we still want what is contrary to God's commands. He acts in a way that is subtle and seductive to draw us step by step away from God and toward the fulfillment of human fleshly desires and needs.

The Devil Is 100 Percent Evil

The devil is pure evil. There is nothing good about him. None of his purposes are good.

Now, the devil can bring good things

into our lives as temptations to ensnare us. He can use something positive as a trick to hide his true intention of producing something negative. That's the purpose behind every temptation.

The devil doesn't say, "I'm going to tempt you to become an alcoholic." No, the devil says, "My, doesn't that drink look good — the color, the shimmer of the ice, the warm feeling people have as they drink, the little umbrella or cherry stuck in the top? Just try one. You'll like it."

The devil doesn't say, "I'm going to lead you into an affair that will destroy your marriage." No, the devil says, "Isn't that a fine-looking person? Doesn't that person seem interesting? Wouldn't you like to spend a little more time getting to know that person?"

The devil can set up a series of good things to lead you down the path he desires for you to walk — a path that is away from God and toward self. The devil doesn't really care how much good you experience as long as you become so wrapped up in that good feeling or good time that you fail to see that your life is about to go over a cliff.

Good things can blind us to the real intent of the devil. We must never lose sight of the truth, however, that the devil is 100 percent evil. He is out for our complete destruction. He has no capacity to give us a blessing that has any eternal benefit associated with it.

The Devil Never Gives Up His Pursuit of Us

You will never fully eliminate the devil's temptation from your life. No matter how mature you may become spiritually, he still has access to you.

The devil does not give up stalking you, especially if you are a Christian. God's Word tells us, "Be sober, be vigilant; because your adversary the devil walks about like a roaring lion, seeking whom he may devour" (1 Peter 5:8).

The devil is like a wild animal, always stalking its prey, always seeking to strike paralyzing fear into that victim with a loud roar.

It is not in the devil's will to stop stalking us.

It is not in the devil's will to stop roaring at us in an effort to instill fear in us.

The only people who don't find themselves under satanic attack are those who are so totally controlled by the devil that they no longer feel guilt or have any conviction about a temptation.

No Immunity

There will never be a point at which you cease to be attacked. There is no plateau of spiritual maturity that keeps you immune from temptations.

Satan did not leave Jesus after he tempted Him in the wilderness. He showed up again in Nazareth, attempting to entice those who knew Jesus from His childhood to throw Him over the edge of a cliff when they took offense at what Jesus preached and taught. (See Luke 4:16–30.)

Satan showed up again in the body of a man filled with a "legion" of demons on the east bank of the Sea of Galilee (Mark 5:9).

Satan showed up in the public attacks that came again and again to assault Jesus' credibility and authority.

Satan showed up in the Garden of Gethsemane, the court of Herod, and the judgment hall of Pilate.

Satan was persistent in his attempts to get Jesus off track. Even though he failed to get Jesus to bow down to him, Satan attempted again and again to get Jesus just one degree off course — to stray just a little from God's purpose for Him.

Satan was always present, seeking any way he could to undermine what Jesus said or to thwart what Jesus did. His ultimate goal was to entice Jesus to say no to the Cross. He never gave up on that goal — he was focused on it until the moment that Jesus declared, "It is finished," and died on the cross. Satan might have thought that he had succeeded in ending the life and ministry of Jesus at that point, only to know with shattering certainty that his fate was fully sealed the instant Jesus rose from the grave.

Satan knows that once you have accepted Jesus as your Savior, you are sealed by the Holy Spirit as God's child forever. There's nothing he can do to rob you of your eternal home in heaven. You are secure in the work that the Holy Spirit has accomplished in your eternal spirit.

Satan also knows that there is nothing he can do to remove the Holy Spirit from your life once you have accepted Jesus. He cannot separate you from God's loving presence. As Paul wrote to the Romans: "Neither death nor life, nor angels nor principalities nor powers, nor things present nor things to come, nor height nor depth, nor any other created thing, shall be able to separate us from the love of God which is in Christ Jesus our Lord"(Rom. 8:38–39).

I often hear Christians pray to invite God's Spirit to join them. The truth is, we don't need to invite the Lord to come into our presence. We are always in His presence! We are never apart from Him.

So why doesn't the devil just give up on you if you are eternally secure in Christ Jesus?

His goal is to keep you from winning souls, from using your spiritual gifts to bless the body of Christ, and from doing God's work — all of which can result in diminishing your reward in heaven. Satan continues to come after you to undermine what you say and do so that your influence for Christ on this earth will be weakened or ineffective. It is for that reason that he continues to seek every way possible to discourage you, cause you to live in depression and oppression, make your life miserable and less fulfilling, fill your mind with doubts, and assault you with all manner of sickness, tragedy, and crises.

The Devil Has a Plan of Attack

The devil has a deliberate, willful plan against your life. He has a goal: to destroy your body, mind, or spirit, or all three. His purpose in doing this is to keep God's purposes from you, deny God the glory He might receive from your life, and ultimately destroy you. He seeks to replace God with himself in your life.

The devil desires not only to destroy what you have — your possessions, your career, your family, your reputation in the community. He seeks to destroy who you are. He wants to demolish your character. He seeks to destroy your peace, joy, happiness, contentment, enthusiasm for life, willingness to take godly risks, generosity, and all other emotional states that are healthy or good.

The devil has attacked every believer who has ever lived. You are no exception. As long as you are alive and the devil exists, you will experience spiritual attacks.

The Nature of a Spiritual Attack

What is a satanic attack? Here is the definition to which we will refer throughout this book:

A satanic attack is a deliberate, willful, intentional, and well-designed act intended to bring harm to a person in any way — physical, mental, economic, relational, or spiritual.

Satan's Objectives

What are the objectives of a satanic attack? He has four:

1. Satan seeks to draw us away from God. That's always his ultimate goal.
2. Satan seeks to thwart us in God's purpose and plan for our lives. He seeks to get us off track and out of the will of God for our lives.
3. Satan seeks to deny God the glory, honor, and praise due Him as we live godly lives of faith and trust in Him.
4. Satan seeks to destroy us — literally and eternally.

The Limitations of Satan's Power

Just as important as knowing who Satan is and what he is up to, we also must recognize the limitations of Satan's power over us. We must have a clear understanding of what Satan can and cannot do in our lives.

As I have stated previously, Satan cannot reverse our salvation. He cannot snatch us out of God's eternal arms. He cannot ever separate us from God's love or put us into a position that is beyond God's reach to care for us, protect us, provide for us, or deliver us.

The devil cannot overcome or negate the work of the Holy Spirit in our lives. He cannot keep us from receiving any blessing that God desires for us to have.

What can Satan do?

The devil does have the power to attack us and tempt us. He has the power to deceive us and oppress us. In so doing, he has the power to

- destroy the quality of our lives. The devil has the power to send sickness and injury our way, to affect our physical, emotional, mental, and financial well-being and our relationships.
- attack our peace and our joy. The devil has the power to send agitation into the calm waters of our lives. He can stir up trouble for us and cause us to find ourselves in turmoil.
- use unbelievers or weak believers to harm us physically, but more often, in the things they say and do that undermine our reputations.
- bring confusion, anger, and frustration into situations and relationships — often for no apparent reason. The

devil is a master at causing misunderstandings.

- decrease our witness for Christ on this earth and diminish our reward in heaven.

We Cannot Defeat the Devil in Our Own Strength

We cannot defeat the devil by human intellect, cleverness, or force of personality. Defeating the devil is the work of Jesus Christ alone, and that work has been accomplished on the cross.

The Scripture never tells us to go out and take on the devil — to seek him out and pick a fight with him. The truth of God's Word is that the war has already been won.

Rather, God's Word urges us to resist the devil. We are to stand firm and withstand his clever tricks that are aimed to entice us and get us off balance, interrupt our stride, and move us to partake of things and experiences that are contrary to God's plan and purpose for our lives.

God's Word also admonishes us to live in God's loving arms, not Satan's grip. We must place our focus on living in Christ and experiencing the power of Christ in us.

We are never to become so consumed with fighting the devil or engaging in spiritual warfare that we lose sight of the fact that we belong to God almighty — He is our Source, He is our Victor, He is our Ally at all times, He is our Strength and Supply, and He is our Protector and Deliverer.

Our stance must always be, "I cannot defeat the devil. But I can resist him and trust Jesus Christ to defeat him." We must declare as the apostle Paul declared, "I can do all things through Christ who strengthens me" (Phil. 4:13).

The wonderful message of the New Testament is this: "Christ in me and I in Christ." We must never lose sight of that glorious, empowering truth. Our enemy is strong. But he pales in comparison to the awesome power and majesty of the Lord Jesus Christ.

3

The Outcome of the Battle

The story is told of a little boy who came into his mother's kitchen and announced to her, "That was a good fight."

The mother looked at her little boy. His shirt was torn and dirty; his jeans were ripped at the knee; he had a black eye and a big scrape on his elbow. "What was so good about it?" she asked.

He replied, "I won."

The Bible tells us that we are to fight the good fight of our faith. (See 1 Timothy 6:12.)

What makes it a good fight?

We are on the winning side.

In any conflict with the enemy of our souls, we must remember at all times — the devil is a defeated foe; Jesus is the Victor.

"But," you may say, "I'd rather not fight. I'd rather avoid a conflict."

We should miss every fight we possibly can. At the same time, we must recognize that we cannot sidestep some issues. Some situations and difficulties are cast upon us without any cause, desire, or provocation on our part.

In the last chapter I shared with you my experience with a recent eye surgery. Was there anything I might have done to avoid those dark, painful days?

"Well," you may say, "you could have said no to the surgery."

Yes, but that thinking relies on hindsight. Unless there are principles of God that we have violated and, therefore, lessons that we can learn and apply to the future, there's very little value in hindsight. Let me repeat that — unless you can look back on a situation and say, "I violated a principle of God in that case and the result was a negative outcome," there's little value in hindsight. There's nothing really to be learned or gained. Many people, however, use hindsight as a response to the external physical attacks of the devil in a wide variety of situations.

The central question we must ask is always this: "Who is in control?"

If you perceive that you are in control of your life and any particular situation, you are in trouble. Why? Because you can't possibly control everything in life or have the wisdom to know what to do in every situation for all people involved. You are a human being prone to failure and to limitations in judgment, power, and ability.

If you believe that life happens at random, you certainly won't be comforted. If life unfolds haphazardly, you have nothing you can count on — there's little use in planning, preparing, learning, or adapting. Furthermore, there's little meaning to life.

But if you understand that God is in control of all things and that life is unfolding according to His master plan and purpose, then you have to look at what happens in your life and conclude, "God knows all about this. He has allowed this to happen. God is in control of all outcomes. He has a way through this difficulty and a good result at the end of this dark tunnel. God is at work, fashioning all things to His glory. He is going to work all things for my eternal benefit."

Do I believe God is in control at all times and in all situations? Absolutely. I know God is in control of the events in my personal life at all times and in all situations. God is in control of the major events of the world at all times and in all situations.

In the aftermath of the September 11

terrorist attack on the United States, a number of stories were told about people who should have been in the Twin Towers in New York City but were not in those towers because of small and seemingly minor situations. One man went to answer a phone and missed his bus and was fifteen minutes late getting to the building; a woman discovered her child had a fever and needed to be taken to a medically equipped day care center instead of his regular day care, and was thus late going to work; one man stopped to pick up donuts for his office staff and was late; another woman slept through her alarm.

God was in control of those situations and at work in those lives for His purposes to be accomplished in the days, weeks, months, and years after September 11.

But what of those who went to work that morning and died as the two massive skyscrapers imploded? Should we conclude that those people could have avoided dying that day if they had just called in sick and not gone to work? No.

God was no less in control of their lives. We may not understand His plans and purposes for their lives to have ended that morning — we may never understand this side of eternity the fullness of God's plans and purposes for that tragic day. But I assure you of this, God was no less in control. His plans and purposes are unfolding — in His timing, according to His methods, and always in a way that will defeat the devil, produce eternal benefit for His children, and bring Him glory.

Prior to having this eye surgery, I had great confidence that I was to have it. I knew there was a degree of risk, which is true for all medical procedures. But I also knew that I had undergone a similar procedure in the past and it went very well. Furthermore, I had prayed with my associates about my having this surgery, and I felt peace about it. The surgeon to whom I had gone had been highly recommended. Most of all, I had full trust in God as my Great Physician.

I want you to note the central truths I have just stated:

- I had prayed about this surgery and had peace about having it.
- Other believers had prayed with me and felt peace.
- I had done everything I knew to do in the natural to ensure success.
- I had full trust in God to be in control and to accomplish His plans and pur-

poses for my life.

If you are living your life in this way —
praying about every major decision,
walking in the peace of God as you go
about your daily routine, doing what you
know to do to live safely and with common-
sense precautions, and trusting God to be
in control always and to accomplish His
plan for your life — you are living the way
God intends! The attacks that may come
your way are not attacks that you could
have avoided.

The greater question is not "What can
we do to avoid attacks from the enemy?"
but "How are we to respond to such attacks when they come?"

The way in which we respond to the enemy's attacks determines whether

- our faith will be strengthened or weakened
- our witness of God's power and presence in our lives will be greater or
  lesser
- God receives greater or lesser glory
  and praise
- unsaved people are more inclined or
  less inclined to trust in Jesus

42

Unprovoked External and Internal Strikes

The enemy can strike us in many ways. His attacks often surround external circumstances — we are faced with illness, injury, assault, loss of a job, betrayal by a friend, divorce papers from a spouse, a sudden drop in the value of a financial portfolio, a flood or fire destroying our homes, or any of a wide variety of attacks that might threaten our bodies, finances, relationships, careers, or material possessions. For me, this particular attack was a physical attack in my body. It was an attack associated with a surgery. For you, the attack may be something very different. It may be your walking in to work one morning and being told that your job is being eliminated in sixty days. It may be going for a routine medical appointment only to be told after your examination that something seems amiss and more tests need to be run. It may be driving a familiar route to take your children to school and finding yourself in an intersection at the same time as someone who has run a red light.

The external strikes of the enemy can never be avoided 100 percent of the time.

We live in a fallen age. We live in a world in which we are surrounded by sinful men and women. We live in a world in which many of our daily mundane actions and behaviors are subject to systems and circumstances that are not based on God's Word.

External attacks happen. The devil has the power to trip us up, inflict harm upon us, and cause evil to adversely affect our lives. Jesus said that the devil comes to steal, kill, and destroy. In other words, Satan has the ability to do just that — to steal from us, hit us with blows that kill some aspect of life, and destroy the work we are doing.

No one is impervious to the devil's external attacks. We do not have a super-spiritual shield that protects us at all times. We see countless examples of this throughout the Scriptures.

Joseph, the son of Jacob, was marked by God for a very special purpose. Even so, God allowed him to be thrown into a pit by his brothers, sold into slavery, falsely accused by his owner, and tossed into a dungeon.

Elijah was perhaps the greatest prophet of the Old Testament. Even so, God allowed Jezebel to persecute him to the point that he fled to a remote cave where he was fed by ravens and drank from a small brook.

Rahab was marked by God for a special purpose. Even so, God allowed all of her friends and business relationships to crumble with the walls of Jericho and be destroyed.

We can and must recognize that no matter how severe the external attack, God is in control; the devil is not.

And because God is in control . . .

- the attack of the enemy is limited in scope
- the attack of the enemy is limited in duration
- the good that God has planned will be far greater than the results of the attack
- God has planned a benefit that will strike a blow against the devil, bring about eternal blessing to God's children, and bring God glory

You can count on these statements always to be true.

Let me remind you of the story of Job in the Old Testament. Many people think of Job and believe his story is about patience.

We even have the phrase in our English language — "the patience of Job." Job's story, however, is really about a man who experienced a spiritual attack.

At the outset of the story we are told that Job was the most righteous man on the earth in his day. God called him "blameless and upright" and said that there was no one like him in all the earth. God gave the devil permission to afflict Job, and very quickly Satan moved to wipe out all of Job's possessions — his flocks and herds, his house, and then all of his children and servants. Job responded by saying,

The LORD gave, and the LORD has
    taken away;
Blessed be the name of the LORD.
    (Job 1:21)

Then God gave Satan permission to strike Job in his body. Job's physical body erupted in painful boils from the soles of his feet to the crown of his head.

That was not the end of Job's suffering, however. Job also suffered anguish in his soul — his mind, emotions, and spirit. Job's wife suggested that he curse God and die. Job refused. Three of Job's friends came to him supposedly to mourn with him and comfort him. They turned out to be of very little comfort — rather, they accused Job of sin, and when Job upheld his righteousness, they accused him of pride. Job finally said to them,

How long will you torment my soul,
And break me in pieces with words?
These ten times you have reproached me;
You are not ashamed that you have wronged me. (Job 19:2–3)

In the end, Job cast himself upon the mercy of an almighty God. He forgave his friends. And God not only restored Job to health but also restored to him more children — seven sons and three daughters — and greater flocks, herds, and wealth than he had before his affliction.

Throughout this story of Job,

- God limited what Satan could do. Satan might have been given the ability to destroy Job's possessions and afflict Job's body, but he could not lay claim to Job's life or his spirit.
- God limited the amount of time Job suffered. He did not allow Satan to

bring more suffering into Job's life than Job could endure.

- God turned the situation for good, rewarding Job with far more than he had lost.
- God received glory from Job's life. Thousands of years later, we are still talking about how Job maintained his faith and trust in God even in the worst of times. Job proved God's faithfulness and God's omnipotent, omniscient goodness.

Whenever the devil strikes us, we can take heart that God has a purpose in allowing the devil to act. The purpose is a divine one that we may not understand but that, nonetheless, is for our good or the good of others. The grief, suffering, or pain is for a season only. The end result, as we remain faithful to God, will bring glory to Him.

As it became apparent that something about the surgery had gone wrong, I had a knowing deep in my spirit: God is in control of this. God had allowed what had happened. He could have prevented it. He could have instantly healed the damage. But He didn't. Therefore, God had a purpose and plan related to my surgery, and I needed to rest in the confidence that God, who knows all, can do all, and sees the future of all things, was and is in control. His purposes were unfolding according to His master plan for my life, and my response was not to wring my hands or moan, "Why me?" but to continue to stand in faith and declare, "I am in Christ. Christ is in me. God is 100 percent in control. I will trust God for my healing."

In the ensuing weeks, I healed sufficiently so that the surgery could be redone — this time successfully. Some of the nerve damage took months to heal, but it did heal. The more important victory, however, was the victory I experienced in my soul and spirit. And that is where your greatest victory will come as well.

Here's what I discovered:

Even though I could not use my eyes, there was nothing wrong with my mouth or my ears. I could listen to people on the phone and converse with them — encouraging them and being encouraged by them. I may not have been able to preach from a pulpit, but I could pastor nonetheless. I could be a friend.

I could pray. I could use this time to intercede for individual people I knew were in trouble. I could intercede for my church and for the In Touch Ministry that circles the globe. I could cry out to God to save those who were hearing our programs in remote places of the earth.

Not only could I intercede for others, but I had opportunity for unlimited stretches of time to spend with the Lord — listening to Him, reflecting on the lessons He had taught me through the years, and praising Him for the way He had brought me through tremendous times of conflict and pain. God used this time to help me come to valuable conclusions about why He had allowed certain things in my life. I wouldn't trade anything for those precious times of communion with the Lord.

I also sensed as the weeks went by that God was giving me an opportunity for deep physical rest. A friend shared with me about an injury he once experienced. He said, "I learned that sometimes God maketh me to lie down in green pastures." I saw this as a time when the Lord was making me to lie down, to lie low, to cease my going and doing. And over the weeks, I felt a significant renewal of my energy — in fact, until that time, I hadn't realized how weary I was from several years of nearly nonstop traveling and preaching.

And most importantly, I felt a renewal of

my trust in the Lord and a strengthening in my spirit. Even though there was not an immediate reversal of my physical condition, I knew without a shadow of a doubt that God would prove Himself strong on my behalf. I knew He was healing me. I knew He was defeating the devil. I knew I would preach again — and preach better than ever. God restored my hope, strengthened my faith, and renewed my love relationship with Him.

Now, I certainly have no desire to repeat that experience with my eyes. But when I think of all the good that God produced as a result of that experience, I can't help rejoicing. God answered many of my prayers in profound ways. The church and the In Touch Ministry increased rather than decreased during those months. I emerged from the experience refreshed in my soul, strong and energetic in my body, and renewed in my spirit.

Was Satan's hand in all this limited? Yes. Was the suffering just for a season? Yes. Did God turn this to my personal good? Yes. Is God getting the glory for His healing work in my life? I pray that He has, is, and will!

Never lose sight that God is in control of your life — all of your life, all of the time.

51

He has a purpose and a plan that is unfolding as you continue to praise and thank Him, and to trust Him step by step.

Three Things You Can Always Count On

You can always count on these things when the enemy attacks you:

1. You can be certain that God will help you. God is holy, omnipotent, omniscient, and immutable. The Bible tells us, "Behold, the LORD'S hand is not shortened, that it cannot save; nor His ear heavy, that it cannot hear" (Isa. 59:1). The Lord desires to help you. He is waiting for you to ask Him!
2. You can rest assured that the attack will come to an end. No temptation or crisis lasts forever. A temptation may come again in another form, or come again after a period of time, but every temptation has a time limit put on it.
3. You can expect to be stronger in your spirit after you have resisted an attack of the enemy.

52

Never lose sight of the truth that God and Satan are not equals.

Satan is not omnipotent (all-powerful). He is not omniscient (all-knowing). He is not infinite.

God — Father, Son, and Holy Spirit — is omnipotent, omniscient, and infinite.

Too many people seem to think that God and Satan are in a tug-of-war, one pulling one way toward good and the other pulling in the opposite direction toward evil. While God and Satan are opponents, they are not equals. Satan is a created being, a finite creature. God is the infinite Creator. There's no comparison in their power, majesty, or glory.

Furthermore, Satan is a defeated foe. His eternal fate has already been established by Christ's death on the cross. He will spend eternity in a lake of fire (Rev. 20:10). Between this moment and the moment that Satan is banished forever into that lake of fire, he has been given permission to test the will of man and to tempt mankind. God allows this as part of the tremendous gift of free will that He has given to every man and woman. God desires for us to choose to love Him, accept Jesus as Savior, and follow Jesus as Lord. But if a person willfully and consciously chooses not to receive Jesus, God will allow that person to make such a choice.

Satan seeks to take to hell with him every human being he can entice into turning away from God's free offer of salvation. That is the motivation behind every spiritual attack. Satan is seeking to turn a person away from God and toward himself. He is attempting to lead that person, in chains of bondage to sin, all the way to eternal damnation if he can.

Jesus, however, secures and seals us by the power of His Holy Spirit so that the devil can never completely destroy believers in Him.

In that supreme truth of the gospel we can stand firm against all attacks and snares of the devil.

4

The Enemy's Snares

A preacher once used a large spool of thread to teach a lesson to a group of children about the way the devil works. He asked a strong-looking ten-year-old to join him on the platform. The preacher then held up a piece of the thread and asked the young man if he could break the string into two pieces. The boy said, "Sure," took the string in his two hands, and easily broke it.

The preacher then asked the children, "Do you think I could tie up a person with this spool of thread so that the person was unable to break free?"

Most of the children shook their heads and said no. A few had a look on their faces that said, *Well, maybe.* None of the children, however, said they thought it was a certainty that the preacher could use the spool of thread to tie up a person.

The preacher then asked for a volunteer to be tied and a volunteer to do the tying. Another strong-looking ten-year-old quickly volunteered to be tied up. A seven-year-old girl volunteered to do the tying. The preacher instructed the ten-year-old to hold his hands together, and then he showed the seven-year-old how to begin to wrap the boy's wrists together with the thread. "Keep wrapping the thread around his wrists while I talk," the preacher said. "We'll see how you are doing in five or ten minutes."

The preacher went on to illustrate a couple of other truths about obedience and trust, and then he came back to the two children with the thread. The little girl had used the entire spool of thread.

"All right," the preacher said to the boy, "now try to break loose."

The boy wiggled and struggled and grimaced as he tried to pull his hands apart, all to no avail. Finally he gave up, and the preacher cut his hands loose from the thread with a large pair of scissors.

"Do you see how the devil works?" the preacher said. "This strong young man was tied up because one round of thread was added to another and to another and to another. Round and round and round the thread was spun. All the while this fine young boy probably thought, *I can break loose*. But in the end, he was trapped. That's the way Satan works in our lives. He feeds us one lie after another and another until finally we can't tell the truth from a lie. He gets us to think one bad thought after another until finally we find ourselves trapped by bad thoughts. He gets us to do one little sin after another — tell one little lie, cheat in one little way, steal one little thing — until finally we are so caught up in our little sins that we can't break loose."

The New Testament refers to the "snare" of the devil — his purpose is to entrap us, catch us off guard, and trip us up. He does this not in an obvious way, but in a subtle and deceiving way. The apostle Paul referred to the devil as wily or crafty (Eph. 6:11).

Much of the time the devil ensnares us one small lie at a time. If he told us a whopping lie, we'd recognize him for the liar he is. He chooses to tell us small lies that are just one degree away from the truth.

He feeds us one little doubt at a time. He brings one little thought of accusation into our remembrance. He clouds the issue so that it appears just a little gray — not clearly black or white.

When a person admits to me, "I don't know why I do what I do," or "I just can't seem to control the way I respond to life,"

I know immediately that this person has been ensnared — he has fallen victim to the devil's crafty manipulations. The devil has tied up the person one round of thread at a time.

The devil sets these schemes or snares against us:

- Debate
- Division
- Doubt
- Deception

The Snare of Debate

Satan always attempts to engage us in conversations that are loaded with "but" and "if" statements. He continually seeks to place conditions and qualifiers on who God is, who you are, and how you might relate to God or other people. The truth of God has no buts, no ifs, no qualifiers or disclaimers.

If you find that you are in a conversation in which a person continually interjects "but" and "what if" and "but what about," recognize that the devil is using that person — not for an honest discussion aimed at getting to the truth of an issue, but a debate solely for the pleasure of disagreement. The person may claim to enjoy a good argument or to like the process of verbally sparring. In the end, however, nothing positive or productive is accomplished. The person may walk away feeling as if he has a little more power or control over you, but in truth, he has only spouted words that brought about confusion, anger, resentment, and doubt. Nothing good comes from any debate that gets tied up or ensnared in a cycle of justifications and speculations.

You can't win a debate with the devil.

Walk away. Say to the person who attempts to debate with you, "Maybe we can discuss this some other time."

If the debate is one the devil seeks to have with you privately in the recesses of your mind, say to the devil, "I'm not discussing this with you." No buts . . . no ifs . . . and no debate.

The Snare of Division

The devil always seeks to divide people. Consider for a moment the state of the world today. Our world is in turmoil as the result of wars and rumors of wars! People are divided against people. There's rebellion against authority in every culture. Conflict and upheaval and political unrest are prevalent. Anarchy and tyranny cause child to betray parent and friend to betray friend. Families are fighting within themselves. Tribal groups are fighting tribal groups. Nations are fighting nations. Groups of nations are fighting terrorists embedded in dozens of nations.

The devil actively seeks to separate husbands and wives, parents and children, employers and employees. He seeks to destroy friendships and divide churches. The devil seeks to cause division in any ministry outreach, and especially so, it seems, in outreaches aimed specifically at presenting the salvation message to the lost in the darkest regions of the world.

Years ago a man told me, "When you begin to take the gospel of Christ overseas, you will experience spiritual attacks in a way you have never experienced them before because when you expand overseas, you will be invading Satan's strongholds. You will be moving into areas where people are in darkness and bondage, having never heard about the saving power of Jesus Christ."

At the time he said this, I thought, *I'll remember that.* Well, I remember it very well to this day because he was right. The devil most certainly did not want us on turf he already thought was securely under his control!

It is critically important in defeating the devil that we continually seek to unite with and remain united with believers who truly are seeking to follow and serve Christ Jesus. We must become yoked with those who are joined to Christ.

We must be very clear on one point: brothers and sisters in Christ are not our enemies. Genuine, committed, Bible-believing Christians who are part of a Christian denomination other than the one to which we belong are not our enemies. We need to recognize that the devil attempts to blind us and deceive us so that we will become divided and begin to war against one another rather than against him! The real enemy is the devil and his forces acting behind the scenes in every case of spiritual assault.

Words of Accusation

The foremost tactic that the devil uses in dividing people is accusation. The Bible refers to the devil as "the accuser of our brethren, who accused them before our God day and night" (Rev. 12:10).

Accusation breeds distrust, anger, hatred, emotional pain, rejection, resentment, and bitterness. Nobody likes to be around somebody who is accusing him or criticizing him all the time. We run from people who do that. We try to put as much space between ourselves and the other person as possible. That's division!

What Unites Us?

If accusation divides us, what unites us? The love of God. Again, let me remind you of what the apostle Paul wrote to the Romans:

> Who shall separate us from the love of Christ? Shall tribulation, or distress, or persecution, or famine, or nakedness, or peril, or sword? . . . Yet in all these things we are more than conquerors through Him who loved us. For I am persuaded that neither death nor life, nor angels nor principalities nor powers, nor things present nor things to come, nor height nor depth, nor any other created thing, shall be able to separate us from the love of God which is in Christ Jesus our Lord. (Rom. 8:35–39)

Words of love and acceptance in Christ

Jesus produce the exact opposite of accusations. Words of love and acceptance generate trust, joy, peace, togetherness, and an open and tender sharing of emotions, dreams, and goals. Those who express the love of Christ to us are people we want to be around. We seek them out and try to become close to them. We allow the love of Christ to cover many of our differences, faults, and tastes, and in doing so, we find that we are able to communicate better, work together, and achieve common goals much more efficiently and with greater quality. That's unity!

The Snare of Doubt

Another of the devil's snares is doubt. If Satan can get you to doubt God's presence, God's love for you, God's forgiveness, God's purpose for you, or God's commandments, he is well on his way to getting you to yield to his temptation. The devil seems to specialize in several categories of doubt.

Doubts About God's Word
Here are just a few of the devil's more popular lines:

"The Bible was written thousands of

years ago to people who lived in the Middle East. This is a different time and culture. Some of the products and technologies and social systems weren't present in Bible times. People back then didn't know what we know today. You have to pick and choose what you read from the Bible. Not everything in the Bible applies to us today where we live."

"The Bible was written by human beings who were subject to making mistakes. How can you know this is really what God commands? After all, the Bible was written by different authors over hundreds of years. Each author had a particular point of view or ax to grind. They lived in different political times and sometimes in different places. You can't take at face value what some of them said. You have to read what seems right to you and discard the rest."

"The Bible is just for Jews and Christians. What about all the other people and their religions? Surely you don't think the Bible is the only book of truth."

"So much of the Bible is just symbolic. All that about the Garden of Eden in Genesis — that doesn't have anything to do with science. And all those symbols in the book of Revelation? How can you know with certainty that everything between

Genesis and Revelation isn't also symbolism?"

"The Bible is a series of stories, and you have to take from stories what you can get from them. They aren't real. The people weren't real. The situations weren't real. It's all fiction."

"There are exceptions to every rule. God surely doesn't mean this in such an absolute way, for all people all the time."

"Everybody has to interpret the Bible for himself. There's no one interpretation that can be trusted."

The truth is, the Bible does relate to us today. All of the authors wrote under the inspiration of the Holy Spirit. He doesn't make mistakes, and He is always timely and eternal. The Bible applies to people in all cultures, all generations, all races, and all situations, circumstances, and social stratas. The Bible is about real people, places, and things — archaeologists are revealing more and more about the accuracy of the Bible. The Bible is the most studied and researched book in the history of mankind, and what it says has been shown to be true again and again. The commandments of the Bible are the absolutes of God — His opinions on sin, judgment, righteousness, obedience, forgiveness, and holiness have not changed and will not change.

When you begin to discount or dismiss the Word of God, you'll find that there's no end to discounting it or dismissing its value. On what basis can you say that some of the Bible is true but other parts aren't? On what basis can you say that you believe some of the miracles but not all of the miracles? On what basis can you say that the love of God is good to believe but the justice and righteousness of God aren't good to believe?

The devil often frames doubt in questions. He generally doesn't come at you and say, "God's Word isn't true." Rather, he says, "Does God's Word really say . . . ?" or "Is that really the right interpretation of that verse?"

Through the years countless people have told me that they have a different interpretation of a particular verse or passage, and amazingly it's always an interpretation that allows them to believe what they already want to believe so they can live the way they want to live — and the way they want to live is nearly always a way that holds the least amount of pain, effort, self-denial, and discomfort! They have decided that life should be easy and that no decisions should have terrible or eternal negative consequences. Therefore, anything in God's Word that calls upon them to make a difficult choice or a hard decision — and especially anything in God's Word that might spell out a decision related to eternal consequences — is given a "different interpretation."

People sometimes ask me, "What do you believe about . . . ?" and they'll name a particular topic or question. I respond, "Let's read what God's Word says." I open the Bible and let the person read aloud a particular passage. The person very often remarks, "Well, I know that's what the Bible says, but there are different opinions on what that means."

There's ultimately only one "different opinion," and that's the devil's opinion. When God says, "Thou shalt not," He means, "Thou shalt not." We can try to define *shalt* and *not* every which way we know, but the command is still, "Thou shalt not." The only different opinion is, "Thou may," and that includes the provision, "Thou may without any negative consequence." That's the devil's opinion.

If you find yourself having to manipulate the interpretation of a very straightforward commandment of God in order to justify your opinion, you're walking on a slippery path. When God says, "Don't do it," He means, "Don't do it"! He doesn't say, "Only certain people are not to do it," or "Only some of the time will there be a negative consequence if you do this," or "This is My opinion right now about not doing this, but centuries down the line, it will probably be acceptable to do this." No. God's commands are very clear. They are very precise. And they are absolute.

The devil asked Eve, "Has God said . . . ?" And when that didn't work, he said, "Surely God didn't mean . . ." He comes at us with the same tactic. He wants us to wonder if God has really spoken on a particular matter. And then if we discover that He has, the devil wants us to question God's meaning.

If the devil can get you to misinterpret God's Word that addresses a particular need or situation, he knows that you are just one step closer to yielding to that temptation.

Doubts About Your Relationship with God

Satan also attempts to encourage you to doubt your personal relationship with God. The devil says:

"Are you really saved? If you were really saved, you wouldn't . . ."

"Do you really have an eternal home in heaven? Are you sure that if you die today, you'll go to heaven?"

"If you are really secure in Christ, then why do you feel so insecure? Surely a secure person wouldn't . . ."

Questions and statements such as these are aimed at one goal: to get you to wonder if you really are saved and that your identity is in Christ. Again, a key message of the New Testament is "Christ is in me, and I am in Christ." The devil will do his utmost to test that central truth of your relationship with Christ Jesus.

When Jesus was baptized, He experienced a strong affirmation from heaven. The Bible tells us the heavens were opened, the Holy Spirit descended on Jesus in a physical manifestation as if a dove was descending upon Him and enveloping Him, and then a voice from heaven said, "You are My beloved Son, in You I am well pleased." (See Luke 3:21–22.)

Immediately after this experience, the Holy Spirit led Jesus into the wilderness to a time of fasting and prayer, and temptation by the devil. What were the first seven words out of Satan's mouth? "If You are the Son of God."

The devil came at Jesus with a question that had a built-in kernel of doubt. If he could get Jesus to question who He was, he might get Jesus to question everything else He believed and sought to do.

The devil comes at you with the same tactic. He tries to get you to question your relationship with Christ Jesus. And to do this, the devil seems to tell three main lies:

Lie #1: Saved people don't sin. Furthermore, they don't have any desire to sin, and they aren't tempted. The truth is that saved people do sin from time to time. They still are human and live in fleshly bodies with natural desires. Every person is tempted.

Lie #2: Some sins are beyond forgiveness — either because the sins are so great in magnitude or because they are repeated so often. God's Word tells us that when we confess our sins to God, He is faithful in forgiving our sins and cleansing us from all unrighteousness. (See 1 John 1:9.) God's mercy and patience with us are beyond measure.

Lie #3: God gets weary of people who sin and repent repeatedly, and He eventually stops forgiving their sins. The truth is that God may chastise us and discipline us when we develop a habit of sinning, but God does not abandon us or cease to forgive us. He continues to prod us toward the way of righteousness so that we will make right choices and reap godly rewards.

Some of the most miserable people I know have been saved by the grace of God but have begun to buy in to these lies and doubt their salvation.

When people express to me that they doubt their salvation, I often ask them to tell me how they accepted Christ and on what basis they accepted Him. They nearly always tell me the truth of what happened: they accepted that Jesus died on a cross for their sins. They received what He did on the cross as being on their behalf. They believed that Jesus was and is the Son of God. They were saved according to their belief in Christ, not on the basis of the good deeds they might have done in their lives.

I generally respond, "That's the way I got saved too! But I'm still saved. What happened to change your mind about your salvation?"

They sometimes claim they have committed an unpardonable sin — a sin they think is very grievous. They often admit that they just don't feel saved.

A person who is still concerned about his sin has not committed an unpardonable sin, no matter how grievous or great the sin may be. The person who needs to be concerned is the one who is not concerned about his sin; in fact, the person is not even interested in reading a book such as this that might talk about his sin.

Furthermore, salvation isn't based upon a feeling, and it isn't assured on the basis of a feeling. Salvation is based upon an act of your will in receiving what God has graciously offered to you! Salvation is the work of the Holy Spirit — forgiving you, cleansing you, and sealing you in Christ Jesus forever. Emotions come and go. They rise and fall. Salvation isn't rooted in emotion.

Finally you didn't save yourself, and you can't unsave yourself. You cannot undo what the Holy Spirit has done in you, and it doesn't really matter what you feel on any given day.

Now, if you don't feel close to God, it isn't because He left you. You left Him! Turn back to God! Do the things that move you closer to Him. Spend more time reading His Word. Spend more time in prayer, especially in thanksgiving and praise. Spend more time in church hearing the Word preached and singing praise songs with other Christians. Go on retreats to be with other believers, talking about the Lord and studying His Word.

If you have sinned, confess it to the Lord, and ask His forgiveness. Also ask Him to help you not to yield to temptation in the future. Daily ask the Holy Spirit to guide you and direct you away from sin and on to the paths that He desires for you to walk.

If you don't believe you were ever genuinely saved — perhaps you were baptized as a child or joined a church without making a personal confession of sin and receiving God's forgiveness — go to the Lord today and pray,

Heavenly Father, I am a sinner. I need Your forgiveness. I accept what Jesus did on the cross as being for me. I receive Jesus Christ, Your only begotten Son, as my Savior. I ask You to cleanse me of my sin and to fill me with Your Holy Spirit.

I have no doubt that if you pray that prayer with sincerity and humility, God will save you and give you the gift of eternal life, just as Jesus said: "For God so loved the world that He gave His only begotten Son, that whoever believes in Him should not perish but have everlasting life" (John 3:16).

Consider what happens if you doubt your salvation.

If you think you are lost, how can you trust God to help you overcome temptation?

If you think you are lost, how can you witness effectively about Christ to another person?

If you think you are lost, how can you rely upon God to deliver you from evil and direct your steps every day so that you live in a way that is pleasing to Him?

Doubts About Your Christian Life

Satan will try to get you to doubt any number of aspects of your Christian life. He often focuses on baptism. He'll point to the discrepancy in the methods used in baptism. He'll say, "You don't need to be baptized. Why, these Christian people can't even agree on what baptism is all about. Some of them sprinkle, some of them pour water over you, and some of them immerse you in water." The truth is, Jesus spoke of the great importance of being baptized by "water and the Spirit." (See John 3:5.)

Satan will try to get you to doubt the importance of going to church. He'll say, "It's just an organization. You won't like many of the people there. You don't have to belong, and even if you join, you don't need to attend regularly." The truth is, the Bible tells us not to forsake coming together with other believers. (See Hebrews 10:25.)

Satan ultimately will try to get you to doubt any and every aspect of the Christian life so that you will devalue, dismiss, or diminish the importance of the most basic Christian disciplines: offering thanksgiving, praise, and prayer; reading and studying the Bible; attending church; giving tithes and offerings; witnessing about Christ Jesus; and using your spiritual gifts to bless others. Why? Because Satan knows that if he can cause you to fail in one area of your Christian life, you will become weak. You'll lose your joy and inner peace. You'll be less likely to use your faith to trust God in difficult times. And over time, you'll falter and begin to withdraw from the greater body of Christ. When you do that, you become less effective for Christ in this world — and that's just what the devil wants! If he can't keep you from coming to Christ in the first place, he'll at least try to keep you from being an effective witness for Christ.

Consider some of the doubts Satan attempts to instill in God's people:

- "Has God really called you into the ministry or commanded you to engage in this particular opportunity to extend the gospel? If so, surely you . . ."
- "If God has called you to do that, you'd be more successful at it . . ."
- "Who do you think you are, attempting to live this way? Everybody knows . . ."
- "What good is all this church stuff anyway?"
- "What difference will your little contribution make?"

All of these doubt-instilling statements and questions are aimed at drawing you away from God, thwarting His purposes for you, diminishing His glory in you and through you, and destroying your witness for Christ!

The Snare of Deception

Deception is a lie about the true reality of something. Deception occurs when we believe things are good, but they aren't;

76

when we believe things look hopeless, but they aren't; when we think something is true, but it isn't; when something looks too good to be true and turns out not to be good at all. Deception is perhaps the devil's foremost snare. The ultimate eternal demise of the devil is described in Revelation with these words: "The great dragon was cast out [of heaven], that serpent of old, called the Devil and Satan, who deceives the whole world" (12:9).

The lies of the devil always have a ring of truth to them. The best counterfeit is always as close to the authentic item as possible. The same for the best lie — it's just one degree from the truth. The devil will tell us that we should "mostly" do what is right. The devil is quick to tell us, "You can't always do what's right. No person is 100 percent right or wrong. No issue is black or white. Life is a mix of good and bad. Life has a lot of 'gray' when it comes to behavior. People have good traits and bad traits. You just need to try to have more good than bad, but a little bad is normal."

The truth is that God always calls us to holy living. God doesn't want us to settle for, tolerate, entertain, or adopt any degree of bad, evil, or spiritual darkness.

Here are two prominent lies of the devil:

1. "You don't have time for that." The devil delights in telling us how busy we are — indeed, we are too busy to listen to God, to read His Word, to pray, or to attend church. He tells us, "You can do all that later. Now is the time to make money, to pursue pleasure, to forge relationships. You're just too busy for spiritual things." Sometimes, he leads us to become wrapped up in good works that have no eternal benefit, and then, the deception is even more potent: "You're busy, but you're busy doing good things. You don't need Christ or the church — you're doing good things that are just as valuable or more valuable than serving God."

2. "Don't think about tomorrow." One of the clever tactics of the devil is to keep us focused on today. He tells us, "Don't worry about tomorrow! Don't think about what might happen. Live for the moment. Live for the experience you can have now."

You are wise to ask yourself about any opportunity, decision, choice, or temptation you face, *Where does this road lead? Where might I end up?*

If we could see the final outcome of sin, we'd never engage in the first act of any sin. Sin leads to death, destruction, and a diminishing of every good thing. It destroys relationships, reputations, and the opportunity to reap great blessings. It hinders growth and keeps us from fulfilling our God-given destiny. It destroys inner peace, joy, and feelings of deep satisfaction. It diminishes self-worth and dashes hopes, dreams, and goals. Sin shackles and limits us in ways that cause us to retreat into ourselves and to hide from the world.

The devil often holds out to a young person this lie: "This might happen to some people, but it won't happen to you." That's deception! Sin sets into motion consequences that may not be reaped this hour or this day or even this year, but the consequences will eventually come to pass! God's Word says plainly, "The wages of sin is death" (Rom. 6:23).

Sin sets into motion the irreversible forces that lead to death — a slow death or a fast death, but death nonetheless. Sin sponsors circumstances that kill the body: disease, accidents, pain, suffering, and limitations. Sin kills relationships through hatred, bitterness, anger, separation, estrangement, divorce, rejection, abuse, slander, abandonment, and distrust. Sin kills reputations and the opportunity for godly influence. It kills opportunities to exercise godly leadership and authority, and it kills opportunities to create or expand ministries that proclaim the gospel.

Don't allow yourself to be deceived about the nature of sin and the consequences associated with it. What God's Word says about sin is true!

The devil said to Eve, "Surely you won't die." (See Genesis 3:4.) He lied.

Lies About Jesus

Perhaps the most insidious lies the devil tells are about Jesus:

- "Jesus isn't the only way to God." This lie is like a malignancy in our world today.
- "All religions are the same — they all lead to God. In the end, everybody who has ever been created will be in heaven. So, there's no need to believe in Jesus or to do anything in response to His death on the cross. Believe what you want to believe; everything will turn out okay in the end."
- "Jesus was just a good man who died a martyr's death. Nobody needs to believe He was the Son of God — just doing some of the good works He told us to do is enough."

80

What Satan says to the unbeliever about Jesus often sounds appealing because it plays on what the unbeliever already wants to believe and the way the unbeliever already wants to live. A life lived according to human desires and man-made philosophies requires little self-discipline, little self-denial, little patience, little strength, little endurance, and little true understanding and wisdom. A life lived in unbelief requires virtually no struggle against temptation. It's an easy road. The problem is, it leads to destruction — loss, depravity, addiction, and devastation in this life — and ultimately eternal death.

The Antidote for Deception — God's Truth!

We sometimes wonder why people act the way they act. We see people who have no relationship with God and no understanding of the Bible, and we say, "Why do they do what they do?" Their actions seem insane to us — without any common sense or rational thinking. The apostle Paul wrote, "If our gospel is veiled, it is veiled to those who are perishing, whose minds the god of this age has blinded, who do not believe, lest the light of the gospel of the glory of Christ, who is the image of God, should shine on them" (2 Cor. 4:3–4). Paul was saying that the devil has blinded those who are unbelievers so they cannot discern the truth. They have no capacity to perceive what is for their eternal benefit, much less their earthly good.

The devil seeks to keep unbelievers in their condition by blinding their minds to the truth. He hates the Word of God, hates the name of Jesus, and especially hates those who believe in Jesus and know the Word! The Word of God will cause people to make choices and decisions that lead to purity, love, and right living. The devil knows that if he can keep people from hearing or reading the Word, he will keep them from making the choices and decisions that will result in their living in and reaping the benefits of righteousness. His first strategy, therefore, is to keep unbelievers blinded to the truth of God's existence, God's love, and God's forgiveness. He desires to keep unbelievers blinded to the truth of God's Word.

Jesus said, "It is the truth that sets a person free." (See John 8:32.) The devil knows that if he can fill a person's mind with doubt and disbelief, that person will not be able to perceive, accept, or act on the truth, and the result is that he will not be set free. He will remain trapped in his sin, guilt, shame, and the consequences of wrong decisions and bad choices.

Truth is the light of the gospel shining in a person's life, showing him who God is, what God is like, and how to relate to Him.

To be able to distinguish truth from a lie is a process we call discernment.

5

Learning to Discern

Five of the saddest words I know are these: "I never saw it coming."

I've heard that statement repeatedly through the years.

Wives have told me about the affairs their husbands have had. They nearly always say, "I never saw it coming."

People have told me about dire financial situations that had them on the brink of bankruptcy or, in some cases, filing bankruptcy. For some reason, they never saw the economic downturn coming — at least not to their businesses or their personal finances.

Men have told me about health problems that they never anticipated would be part of their lives, even though they knew they were doing things that were unhealthful.

Mothers have known for years that their children were growing up, but when an empty nest became a reality, they told me that the depression and feelings of uselessness they felt were totally unanticipated.

The Bible admonishes us to live each day fully — not living in the past or the future. But God never intends for us to walk blindly from day to day. He expects us to discern what He is doing and what He desires. He intends for us to have a capacity to see beneath the surface of life and to expose and analyze the unseen.

Discernment is the ability to judge a situation accurately — to see the full reality of a situation, relationship, experience, or circumstance. It is the capacity to understand accurately and clearly what is, to see the truth of things as they are from God's viewpoint. Discernment for the believer is seeing and understanding as God sees and understands. It is the ability to make godly judgments and right appraisals.

"But," you may be saying, "we're not to judge."

The Bible tells us that we are not to judge people, which means we are not to take upon ourselves the role of passing sentence on other people. We are, however, to judge behavior as being good behavior or bad behavior. We are to know what is right and wrong, good and bad, effective and ineffective, true and untrue. The Bible tells us, "The time has come for judgment to begin at the house of God" (1 Peter 4:17). Believers, especially, are to have sound judgment based upon accurate discernment.

God calls His people to know the "difference between the holy and the unholy, and cause them to discern between the unclean and the clean. In controversy they shall stand as judges, and judge it according to My judgments. They shall keep My laws and My statutes in all My appointed meetings, and they shall hallow My Sabbaths" (Ezek. 44:23–24).

God's Word has very strong words for those who know "the righteous judgment of God" but proceed anyway to "practice such things" — referring to unrighteousness, sexual immorality, wickedness, covetousness, maliciousness, envy, murder, strife, deceit, evil-mindedness, gossip mongering, backbiting, the hatred of God, violence, pride, boasting, the invention of evil things, disobedience of parents, lack of trustworthiness, and all sorts of other unloving, unforgiving, unmerciful behavior. Not only are we not to engage in these practices, but we are not to approve of people who do. (See Romans 1:28–32.)

Four aspects of discernment are vitally important for us to recognize:

1. Discernment between good and evil
2. Discernment between what is real and what is illusion
3. Discernment between what is good and what is best
4. Discernment between our desires and God's plan

Why do we need to have clear discernment in these areas?

Because the enemy attempts to trick us — to deceive us, tempt us, and destroy us — in each area!

We open ourselves up to attacks when we don't recognize evil for what it is, when we don't see the true reality of a situation, when we settle for less than God's best, and when we mistake our desires for God's desires.

1. Discernment Between Good and Evil

Most people know the general principles related to right and wrong. There are occasions, however, when evil can cloak itself in what appears to be good. We all know the children's fable about the wolf that put on sheep's clothing in order to get into a flock of sheep and raise havoc. There are wolves — people functioning with evil intent — who often don the guise of good works and good social standing in order to wreak havoc in the church or in our communities. We need the ability to discern between good and evil.

We especially need to be able to discern the motives and hearts of those who rise to leadership in the church. The apostle Paul wrote at length about this to the church at Corinth. He concluded, "Do not be deceived: 'Evil company corrupts good habits.' Awake to righteousness, and do not sin; for some do not have the knowledge of God" (1 Cor. 15:33–34).

2. Discernment Between What Is Real and What Is Illusion

We need to be able to tell if what we are seeing and hearing is fact or fiction.

A friend once told me about taking her niece to see a live theatrical performance of *Peter Pan*. The little girl leaned over to her aunt during one part of the play and said, "Are those real Indians?" Her aunt realized that they were sitting far enough from the stage that her niece might have thought she was watching a giant-screen television show. She said, "Those are real people, not TV people." Her niece responded, "Yes, but are they real Indians?"

The answer, of course, was no. Not one of the actors was an Indian, and the portrayal of the Indians in the play on stage was not an accurate portrayal of the way Indians generally behave today.

Some opportunities that come our way may appear to be real, valid, and wonderful — only later do we discover that we have been tricked.

Some people may come into our lives and give the appearance of good character — only to be shown later to have had very bad motives.

Some substances may be offered to us under the guise of being helpful or healthful — only to be shown later to have deadly long-term side effects.

We need to be able to discern what is really true.

3. Discernment Between What Is Good and What Is Best

Many a person has failed to receive God's best in his life because he settled for what seemed to be "good."

God does not desire that any person live a so-so, average life. He desires for every person to live an excellent life — morally excellent, spiritually excellent, relationally excellent. It isn't a matter of how much money or material goods a person has — but the degree of love, joy, and peace a person has. It isn't a matter of how much status or fame a person has — but whether a person has excellent health and excellent friendships and family relationships.

Years ago a young man told me that he was planning to ask a certain young woman to marry him.

"Is this God's best for you?" I asked him.

He shrugged his shoulders and said, "Actually, Pastor, I think she may be the only girl who will have me."

I said, "That's not good enough!"

As it turned out, this young man's self-esteem was so poor that the girl he thought would marry him finally got so tired of having to build him up and encourage him that she gave up on their relationship and called off their engagement.

Years passed. I watched this young man develop and grow in his personality, his trust of God, his career, his understanding and application of God's Word, and his prayer life. He became strong and confident. He came to me a second time and said, "I'm getting married."

"Is this God's best for you?" I asked.

"Absolutely!" he said. "At one point in my life I don't think a woman like this would have ever looked my way, but God has prepared me for her and prepared her for me. She's the one!" He said it with such joy in his eyes and love in his heart that I knew he was right!

God doesn't want you to have a mediocre job that you hate getting up and going to every day. He doesn't want you to have an average marriage. He doesn't want you to have just a little bit of peace in your life. No! God desires for you to feel fulfilled and overjoyed in your life. He wants you to experience His highest and best!

4. Discernment Between Our Desires and God's Plan

All of us have to guard against pursuing our own plans and desires, and instead pursue what we know to be God's best for us. In the end, God's plan for us is the plan that will fit us perfectly. It will excite us the most and bring us the greatest feelings of meaning and satisfaction.

A father once said to me, "My son thinks he's going to be an actor. He's going to New York next week to take his chances at making it big."

I asked this man, "Have you talked to your son about whether this is what God has for him?"

"Oh, yes," the man said. "I'm opposed to this. I think it's a long shot that he can make it into the big time. But my son tells me he has prayed about this, and he truly believes God is calling him to be a Christian actor."

I know a number of young people who dream of being in the movies or on stage, and the dreams are just their dreams. They aren't God's desires for them. I didn't know this young man so I couldn't discern God's plan for him. I could only assure the father that I would pray for his son.

As it turned out, this young man had a very successful stage career in New York City, and he became a leader in writing, staging, and acting in Christ-centered plays and pageants across America. His desire and God's desire matched up.

Ask God to reveal His plan to you. Ask Him to show you the talents He has built into your life. Trust Him to show you how to develop those talents and use them to make a difference for Christ Jesus in this world. Don't settle for your own dead-end goals — get in line with God's goals and be all that He created you to be!

Discernment Is a Three-way Key

Discernment is a three-way key — it is a key to understanding God's will, having good judgment, and knowing God's voice.

1. A Key to God's Will

We must have discernment if we are going to live in the will of God. There's too much in our world that seems right, but isn't. There's too much that feels good, but doesn't turn out to be good.

For example, often movies are advertised as family films or are given ratings that imply they are suitable for children to watch. Many parents don't realize, however, that the standards have shifted. A "good" movie may have hidden messages and very vulgar language or bad scenes. Often the message of a film can be what is not said more than what is said. The body language of the actors and the ways in which they dress and act can convey a message that is very much opposed to God's commandments related to sexual purity, honesty, generosity to the poor, and so forth.

Most people don't even think to ask before they go to see a movie, "Is this something God would be pleased for me to see? Is this something that reinforces the values that God desires for me to have in my life?"

No, we don't ask these questions, but we should. There's nothing as important as living in a way that is pleasing to God and that reinforces in us and in our children the principles and commandments of God's Word. Anything that is contrary to God's Word is going to pollute our minds in some way and cause us to become confused about what truly is right and wrong, or acceptable and unacceptable in God's eyes.

"But shouldn't a person know what the world is all about?" you may be asking. "Shouldn't I expose myself to some of the abnormalities and ills of society in order to know how to reach the lost?"

No.

The world needs answers that are rooted in knowing Christ Jesus, not someone who knows a little bit about sin, even vicariously through a movie.

When it comes to things that feel good in our world — the truth is, most of what the devil holds out to us in temptations feels good, at least for a few seconds or minutes. The world says that if something is bright, glitzy, dazzling, and has a good, strong beat to it, it's good. That simply isn't the truth.

Feelings can be very deceptive. They are temporary, often fleeting. What feels good in one minute doesn't necessarily feel good two hours later. The person who lives totally by what feels good is easily swayed and often finds himself on a roller coaster of emotions, going from feelings of "very high" to "very low" so often that he has no stability and, from the standpoint of other people, no reliability.

Much of what the world offers to a person is empty of real substance. I liken it to cereal box value. I enjoy eating cereal for breakfast, but I've realized over the past decade that the boxes seem to be bigger and bigger and have less and less cereal in them. When you take a box from the grocery story shelf, you likely expect a full box of cereal. Take the bag inside the box out of the box and put it next to the box and you'll quickly discover that within the bag of cereal is a lot of air!

The same is true for many experiences the world offers. We need to be able to discern the things that are full of value and the things that are void of all value.

God's Word tells us, "Test all things; hold fast what is good. Abstain from every form of evil" (1 Thess. 5:21–22).

2. A Key to Good Judgment

Discernment is also critical if we are to exercise basic good judgment.

From time to time, I watch infomercials to see what the current trends seem to be in products and marketing. I have been amazed at the variety of devices that are sold under the label "exercise equipment." Thin, fit people, of course, are the ones who are advertising this equipment, and there's always the hook that if you buy in the next ten to fifteen minutes, you'll get bonus items. The pitch is always direct — if you don't buy this, you are losing out on a miracle-producing product.

These infomercials never tell you or show you that overweight, out-of-shape people sometimes have difficulty using the piece of equipment, improper use of some of these devices can cause real injury or pain to out-of-shape people, and the price is going to be increased by at least 20 percent for shipping and handling!

When it comes to exhibiting good judgment, we must take the stand that we don't need to buy something just because it seems interesting, we don't need to go someplace just because we are invited, and we don't need to do something just because we are asked to do it.

3. A Key to Knowing God's Voice

Discernment is perhaps most critical in determining when God is speaking to you. We hear countless voices in a given day — some of them come from people who work with us or live with us or around us; some of the voices are in the media; some of the "voices" are in our memories or in our minds. Do you know the sound of God's voice? The Lord said that He speaks in a still, small voice. (See 1 Kings 19:12.) Few of us ever get quiet enough to hear that voice. The Lord also said that He is our Shepherd, and as His sheep, we will know His voice. (See John 10:4.) Do you recognize God's voice speaking in your heart?

To help us determine if God is speaking to us, or if the voice we are hearing is not of God, we can remember a few points.

97

First, the Lord will never impose on us something that hampers us from using the talents, skills, and resources that He has given to us. Some people have the personal preferences of others imposed on them — they are told what they must or must not wear, how they must speak and act in every situation, or how they must give. Cults are notorious for this. Cult leaders nearly always insist that their followers adopt a particular manner of dress, and a manner of speaking and acting in all situations (which is very often not speaking unless spoken to and not acting without the cult leader's permission), and that they must give all their worldly goods and money to the cult leader.

God desires that we express our talents as creatively and generously as possible for His glory. God desires that we give cheerfully and freely without coercion. God desires that we openly voice our praise and thanksgiving to Him, not giving homage or worship to a human being. God desires that we live in grace, not legalism imposed by the personal preferences of other people. We must be quick to discern if a person is pointing toward God's Word or simply imposing his own mandates under the guise of spirituality.

Second, the Lord will never speak something to us that is contrary to Scripture. No matter how godly or wise the counselor who may be speaking to you, if that person says something that is contrary to what the Bible says, he is speaking totally out of his own opinion, not out of the wisdom of God. To determine if it truly is the Lord who is speaking to you, you need to check the message against God's Word — and not just against one isolated verse that may seem to verify or confirm what you want the message to be. You need to weigh the message you are receiving from God against the whole of God's truth.

Trust the Holy Spirit on a daily basis to show you what to look at and what not to look at; what to eat and what not to eat; what to drink and what not to drink; where to go and where not to go; whom to fellowship with and whom to refrain from association with. Ask Him to show you who genuinely loves you and who is only trying to use you for his own purposes. Ask Him to reveal to you who is preaching the truth and who is preaching something that sounds good but isn't really the truth.

The person who does not discern God's voice or God's will, and is void of sound spiritual judgment as well as sound practical judgment, opens himself up to spiritual attack. Such a person won't know when the devil is whispering in his ear, won't have any basis on which to evaluate choices or opportunities, and won't be able to see down the path to recognize the potential consequences of various decisions. Such a person is also prone to becoming enticed by false teachers and cult leaders who operate under the influence of Satan.

The Importance of Obedience

When God speaks to us to reveal His will and His good judgment, we must be quick to obey. Many people who have had spiritual discernment have not heeded God's directives. When we fail to obey, we lose our keen ability to discern. Our consciences become seared, and our discernment becomes cloudy. Spiritual discernment works fully only when we desire to obey and actually do obey God's directives.

An unbeliever can't have spiritual discernment because he isn't living in relationship with the Holy Spirit who gives discernment.

A believer won't have spiritual discernment if he chooses to sin when he knows God's will and ignores it.

No one can fully obey without the help of the Holy Spirit. Invite the Holy Spirit to help you walk in obedience after He reveals God's will and God's judgments. Pray,

Lord, I trust in You to give me a discerning spirit today. I trust You to guide me. I want to be spiritually sensitive in every situation I encounter. Holy Spirit, prompt me when people ask me a question or speak to me so I might respond with what You desire for me to say. Help me to see with Your eyes and hear with Your ears. Speak to my heart.

The Holy Spirit delights in answering that prayer.

The Ongoing Pursuit of Spiritual Discernment

How might we go about developing greater spiritual discernment?

First, we must recognize that spiritual discernment is something to be desired and sought. Spiritual discernment does not instantly and automatically flood the inner being the moment we accept Jesus Christ as our Savior. The Holy Spirit fills us with His presence, and He is the Author of spiritual discernment, but the ability to discern comes as part of the process of our minds and hearts being renewed.

The psalmist was quick to say, "Teach me good judgment and knowledge" (Ps. 119:66). That must be our prayer as well.

We need to recognize that not everything is seen with physical eyes or heard with physical ears. We must ask the Lord to reveal to us what we need to know that we aren't seeing or hearing with our physical eyes and ears.

What really matters is not what we think we perceive, or what others tell us is the truth, but what God says is the accurate perception and the truth of any situation.

Second, we must rely upon the Holy Spirit to be the Source of truth in us. Jesus taught that the Holy Spirit would be in us, with us, and upon us. The Holy Spirit determines our spiritual gifts, instructs us in the Word of God, empowers and energizes us, and is our Helper in all situations. The Holy Spirit reveals what Jesus would do and say in any given situation, and enables us to discern the truth in all situations.

(See John 14–16.) Above all, the Holy Spirit reveals to us the truly important things of life — the things that are of God and that have eternal benefit. God's Word tells us:

"Eye has not seen, nor ear heard,
Nor have entered into the heart of man
The things which God has prepared for
    those who love Him."
But God has revealed them to us through His Spirit. For the Spirit searches all things, yes, the deep things of God. For what man knows the things of a man except the spirit of the man which is in him? Even so no one knows the things of God except the Spirit of God. Now we have received, not the spirit of the world, but the Spirit who is from God, that we might know the things that have been freely given to us by God. (1 Cor. 2:9–12)

The Holy Spirit resident in you will reveal your sinful motivations, attitudes, and beliefs — He will reveal to you when you sin or are about to sin. How important this is! Too many people like living in denial of their sin. They don't want to confront their motivations or evil tendencies. They also don't want to face their neediness or their dependency upon God.

We must rely on the Holy Spirit if we truly are going to have a renewed heart and mind and be able to develop spiritual maturity so we aren't led around by the devil as if we were on his leash.

Third, we must be willing to study the Word of God. We must seek out God's opinion on every issue. The Bible reveals to us who God is — His thoughts, His desires, His plans and purposes, His ways. The stories of the Old Testament give us wonderful illustrations of God's love and character. The New Testament shows us how a person who is filled with God's Spirit can and must respond to life.

The psalmist knew the tremendous value of God's Word in the development of discernment. He wrote,

Oh, how I love Your law!
It is my meditation all the day.
You, through Your commandments,
    make me wiser than my enemies;
For they are ever with me.
I have more understanding than all my
    teachers,
For Your testimonies are my
    meditation.

I understand more than the ancients,
Because I keep Your precepts.
I have restrained my feet from every evil
way,
That I may keep Your word.
I have not departed from Your
judgments,
For You Yourself have taught me.
How sweet are Your words to my taste,
Sweeter than honey to my mouth!
Through Your precepts I get under-
standing;
Therefore I hate every false way.
Your word is a lamp to my feet
And a light to my path.
(Ps. 119:97–105)

To study God's Word means that you read it regularly, asking God to help you understand and apply what you read. Study also means that anytime you face a major decision, opportunity, or crisis, you turn to God's Word for God's wisdom. You ask the Lord to guide your study of the Scriptures to get the whole of God's instruction on a given matter. Use a concordance to look up key words. Read all the Scriptures related to the topics that address your concern or questions. Open your heart to the Lord, and say to the Holy

Spirit, "Teach me. Show me. Lead me. Direct my reading and studying. I want to know God's highest and best for my life." I have absolutely no doubt that God will answer a sincere and humble prayer for His instruction!

The instruction of the Holy Spirit in our lives is ongoing. We never fully know everything we need to know. We never graduate from God's schooling of us when it comes to discernment. Continue to ask the Lord for guidance. Continue to read and study His Word. You will continue to grow in your ability to discern. As more and more of God's truths are planted into the grid of your mind, the more clearly you will be able to see and hear the messages behind the obvious.

A Gift We Receive by Faith

Discernment is God's gift made available to every believer, but as is true for all gifts from God, we must actively receive this gift and do so by faith. We must ask God to impart His discernment and then believe that He will give it. We must believe that when we ask for God's direction, He will guide us. We must believe that when we ask God to show us what is counterfeit and real, He will reveal all we need to know to make wise and godly choices.

We also need to be patient in waiting for assurance or confirmation that we are discerning correctly. If you have any doubt that God has shown you the reality of a situation, ask God to confirm His revelation to you. Ask Him to bring to light anything that is hidden. Ask Him to cause the motives of a person to be manifested in a way that you, and others, can readily recognize those motives. Ask Him to make clear any aspects of an opportunity or crisis that seem cloudy or in shadows of darkness. The truth of God shines as a very bright light. Ask God to shine His truth on any situation that seems questionable to you.

6

Extinguishing Fiery Darts

A colleague shared with me recently an experience he had while preaching on the mission field in Africa. He had been breaking out in welts periodically for about six months. He kept a food diary but could see no relationship between what he was eating and the outbreak of welts. He asked local residents about various types of foliage that might be blooming or pollinating, but could find no relationship between the plants of the area and the random appearance of welts. Then one day he had a particularly bad outbreak. Rather than be confined to a localized area as they had been in the past, the welts seemed to be all over his body.

He preached that night to a small group gathered in a remote area several miles from the village in which he was living. He had hardly been able to see the dirt path that others had described to him as "the road." A group of about thirty had gathered in a small hut made of thatch, mud, and dung. The only light in the room was provided by a kerosene lamp, which gave just enough light for him to see the eyes of those hearing his message.

He told me, "That night, it seemed to me that I had truly fulfilled the Great Commission of Jesus to take the gospel to the uttermost bounds of the earth. I thought to myself, *If this isn't the uttermost bounds, I don't know what is.*"

Then he told me that he awakened abruptly in the middle of the night. "This was not all that unusual," he said. "The Lord sometimes awakens me in the middle of the night to pray. But this night, when I opened my mouth to begin to praise His name and pray as the Spirit might lead me to pray, I couldn't get out a sound. I could feel welts inside my throat cutting off my air supply."

"What did you do?" I asked.

"I panicked," he said. "I couldn't breathe!"

"That was a real attack of the enemy," I observed. "The devil was trying to stop the ministry there."

"Yes," he said. "I believe you are right on that. But the attack wasn't just against my body."

"What happened?"

"The thought immediately filled my mind, *You are going to die tonight. You have preached in Jerusalem and in Judea and in the uttermost bounds of the earth, and your job is done. Your life is over.*"

"Did you believe that?" I asked.

"For about two seconds I did because I couldn't breathe!" he said. "But the truth of that moment was that I knew God wasn't finished me with yet, and I didn't have any intention of dying that night! I got out of bed and ran immediately from that little two-room place where I was sleeping to a building about twenty feet away. I don't know how I got the energy to run there. I must have been able to get some oxygen. I rapped on their door until a fellow missionary and his wife answered. They began to pray immediately for me, and their teenage son ran to get a missionary doctor in yet another little house about fifty feet away."

"Were you fearful?" I asked.

"I was initially," he replied, "but then I started listening to the prayer of my fellow missionary and his wife. They kept saying over and over, 'You will live and not die. Nothing the enemy sends against you will succeed. You will live and not die. You will live and not die. You will live and not die.'

They kept repeating that statement. I believed more what they were saying to God in prayer than what the devil had whispered in my ear. In my innermost being, I found myself saying silently, *I will live. I will not die tonight. I will live*."

"Did your breathing improve?" I asked.

"Within a minute or two," he said. "By the time the missionary doctor arrived, I was breathing normally. He gave me some antihistamine tablets to take."

"Did you ever have an attack like that again?"

"No. I felt led to buy a different type of water purifier after that experience, and I never had another attack after that night. Something more important happened, however, than my physical recovery."

"What was that?"

"That night was something of a showdown with the enemy. He had launched a major attack against me. I said to the devil later, 'You gave it your best shot to take me out early. I'm putting you on notice that I will not buy in to your lies about death ever again.' "

"Had the devil lied to you before about death?"

"Sure," he said. "Before I went to Africa, I had several bouts of concern and fear about dying in Africa. I imagined all sorts of things."

"So this was about fear as much as it was about welts," I said.

"I believe it was. The welts gave me good cause for fear, but welts alone don't cause fear or thoughts about dying in the uttermost bounds of the earth. The good news that came out of that experience is that I never had welts again, but I also never had another bout with intense fear that I was going to die in Africa. I ministered boldly and without fear in Africa for more than twenty years before God led me to a different place of ministry."

Satan is a stealer of the truth. He may send or use a situation that strikes the body, but he works primarily in the mind.

Fiery Darts

The apostle Paul wrote that we who are in Christ are going to face "all the fiery darts of the wicked one" (Eph. 6:16). God's desire is that we be able to extinguish all the flaming arrows that the devil sends our way.

What are these flaming missiles or flaming arrows?

In the natural, the flaming arrows to which Paul referred were arrows common to Roman battles. They were arrows that had been dipped in pitch and lighted. When these arrows were launched into a group of enemy soldiers, they were a double threat. Not only did the arrow penetrate what it hit, but it could cause fire to spread in the midst of the soldiers. At times in ancient battles, hundreds and even thousands of these arrows might be lighted and launched at the same time. The result was often massive casualties, including fires that could wipe out the soldiers' camps. In such a "rain" of flaming arrows, it was very difficult for a soldier to keep from being hit. And even if he did avoid a direct hit, he had to deal with fire all around him. A barrage of flaming arrows was very effective and very deadly.

In the spiritual, flaming arrows refer to the bombardment of the mind with thoughts, impressions, and impulses that are contrary to God's purposes. These thoughts might be thoughts to do evil. They might be angry thoughts, sinful thoughts, or temptations to sin.

When the enemy unleashes a rain of such thoughts against a person, or against a group of godly people, the results can be devastating unless a person is able to intercept the arrows and quench their fire.

Here are just some of the arrows that the devil may unleash at you:

- Fear — "You have good reason to be afraid right now and always."
- Doubt — "You can't trust God or trust that God will work in this situation for your good."
- Lust — "You need to have your needs met, and this is a fine way to get your needs met."
- Loneliness — "You are alone, you will always be alone, and you, therefore, will always be miserable."
- Jealousy — "You aren't being shown the devotion you deserve, and at the same time, somebody else is getting the devotion that should be yours."
- Rejection — "You are worthy to be rejected and cast aside."
- Guilt — "You should feel guilty about that sin — shame, shame, shame on you."
- Greed or covetousness — "You should have that. You deserve it. You need it."
- Unforgiveness — "You can never forgive that sin, and even if you could, why would you?"
- Anger — "You've been hurt and you

have a right to be angry."

- Discouragement — "You'll never have what you desire or be who you desire to be in this life. Don't even get your hopes up."
- Pride — "You're above all that; you shouldn't have to stoop to accommodate the weakness or poverty of another person."

Any thought or impulse that entices a person to fall victim to the "lust of the flesh, the lust of the eyes, and the pride of life" is a fiery dart! (See 1 John 2:16.)

The Devil's Access

Temptations, doubts, accusations, justifications, and speculations begin in the mind. Our feet, hands, and bodies follow where the mind leads us. It is in our minds that we remember, we understand, we make decisions, we fantasize, and we evaluate truth from fiction. It is with our minds that we believe, we acknowledge God, and we make choices. The battleground with Satan is the mind.

Many people ask, "Does the devil have access to my mind?" Yes.

Can the devil send thoughts into the mind? Yes.

Can the devil speak to the heart? Yes.

Now we need to be very clear on several points.

First, a thought itself is not sin.

Entertaining a thought and acting out a thought can be sinful. Thoughts come — and it is what we do with those thoughts that matters.

Second, the devil does not send the same thoughts to every person. The devil sends thoughts that are tailor-made to the neediness an individual feels. To the person who doesn't have a need for material possessions to bolster his self-esteem, a thought of "You need to buy this or have that" isn't going to take root in the mind. To the person who doesn't feel a need for greater sexual satisfaction, a lustful thought about a person at work isn't going to lodge in the mind. To the person who isn't addicted to alcohol, a message about the benefits of having a drink isn't going to impact the mental habits. The devil knows your area of weakness and need. He crafts his messages specifically for you.

Third, the devil often aims thoughts at things we value as being good or right. He aims his darts at your appreciation for beauty, the value you place on knowledge and competency, or the longing you have for approval, value, and love.

Is there anything wrong with beauty or with appreciating beauty? No.

Is there anything wrong with knowledge, competency, or the acquisition of skills? No.

Is there anything wrong with the need of the human heart to feel love, approval, value, and worthiness? No.

But here's how the devil twists these good things for his evil purposes.

For the person who places a high value on beauty, the devil points out ways in which the person doesn't have beauty in her life. He whispers, "You don't have the beautiful things you like, the lovely home you should have, the beautiful garden estate that you would know how to care for and value." He points out everything that seems ugly or lacking in appeal and plays on the person's desire for beauty.

For the person who has a high regard for knowledge and intellectual ability, the devil points out ways in which the person doesn't have the knowledge or competency in his life that he desires — or he points out the lack of knowledge or competency in a spouse, a friend, or the people with whom the person works. The devil puts a spotlight on all of the mistakes that others are making. The person begins to bemoan the fact that he was denied a college education or the career training he should have had. The devil focuses on the ways in which the person isn't as knowledgeable or competent as he desires to be.

For the person who believes the most important things in life are love, approval, and worthiness, the devil points out all the ways in which people are treating him in unloving, disapproving, devaluating, and degrading ways. The devil says, "You don't have the respect you deserve. You aren't appreciated in the ways you should be appreciated. You aren't given the prominence you should have." The devil points out the lack of love in the person's life because the person places very high value on love and approval.

The devil never points out the abundant blessings of God in your life. The devil always points out what is missing, lacking, or negative. He may point to what is good and right, but it will always be in the context that these things are missing in your life. The devil sends thoughts and impulses that register as "want," "need," and "must have."

The Devil's Strategy

How do the fiery darts of the devil operate in our minds?

First, the devil sends a thought. When that happens, we have a choice — to reject that thought immediately or to entertain it. If we reject the thought, the devil may send another thought — very quickly or sometime later. At times, the thoughts can come into our minds with such a rush that we will feel as if a hundred flaming arrows have been launched against us. We can feel bombarded.

Not long ago a person told me about his experience on his way home. This man worked in Southern California, and he lived about thirty minutes away from his workplace "if the freeways were fairly clear." He usually carried a bottle of water with him in his car, but this day he had forgotten to bring along some water. He told me that no sooner had he pulled out of the parking lot of his company than he saw a billboard for a nice, cold drink.

He said, "I wasn't thirsty when I left the building, but within seconds after seeing that billboard, I was thirsty." Then the man turned on the radio in his car, and the first commercial he heard was for a soft drink. Over the next half hour, this man saw eight billboards or signs about beverages — all of them showing beverages that were ice-cold and thirst-quenching. It seemed to him that everywhere he looked he saw signs for fast-food places and convenience stores where he would be able to buy a cold drink.

He said, "By the time I got home I was so thirsty, I drank more than a quart of water in what seemed like one giant gulp!"

I said to him, "Just be glad you were thirsty for water!"

Although obviously drinking water is not a sin, this is an example of the way the devil hits us with impressions, perceptions, and ideas — one after another, all aimed at a physical, emotional, psychological, or spiritual need. It may be television commercials, radio commercials, billboards, signs, memories, visuals of people who remind us of people we know, and on and on. We can become "thirsty" emotionally and psychologically for everything from alcohol to sweets to nicotine to sex to a new car. The thirst at times can seem insatiable, nagging, insistent, interminable.

The more you entertain a thought aimed at a need you feel, the more that thought looms in your mind until it crowds out all other thoughts.

Second, if you entertain thoughts repeatedly — over days, weeks, or months — the thoughts take root in you and become normal to you. You develop a particular pattern or habit in your thinking. Habitual ideas can become ingrained to the point that a major blast of God's power is required to remove the idea from your mind or alter your habitual pattern of thinking.

The initial thoughts the devil sends to us may be just a "toehold" the first time we entertain those thoughts and dwell on them or fantasize about them. The longer we entertain the thoughts, however, the more likely we are to start making mental plans about how we might act on them. It is then that the toehold of an idea becomes a "foothold." The more we develop plans for acting on a sinful idea or temptation, the more we find that the foothold has become a "stronghold." We come to the place where we feel compelled to try out the idea in our behavior. We have fantasized and imagined what it was like to do something, experience something, or try something for so long that we come to the place where we want to act on that idea more than we want to banish the idea.

Toeholds, Footholds, and Strongholds

The apostle Paul wrote,

For though we walk in the flesh, we do not war according to the flesh. For the weapons of our warfare are not carnal but mighty in God for pulling down strongholds, casting down arguments and every high thing that exalts itself against the knowledge of God, bringing every thought into captivity to the obedience of Christ, and being ready to punish all disobedience when your obedience is fulfilled. (2 Cor. 10:3–6)

Habitual patterns of thinking become strongholds in our minds. Where do these strongholds take root in us? To what do they relate? They are linked to the areas of our perceived greatest need. They are related to our weaknesses.

If Satan is capable of deceiving you, craftily manipulating you, and seducing you to yield to temptation in one area of your life, he's going to come back again and again to that area. He has identified this as an area of weakness in your life. The more times he successfully tempts you in that area, the weaker that area becomes. This area of weakness in you becomes a spiritual stronghold for him! What is weakness in you is a strong place for him to work in your life. Initially the area of weakness may be just a toehold for the devil, but then as you yield to temptation in that area, it becomes a foothold for the devil, and as you continue to yield to temptation in that area, it becomes a stronghold. It becomes a calloused, hardened area of your life. It truly is an area in which the devil gains a strong hold on you!

Most people who are willing to admit that they have yielded to temptation usually identify one or two areas in which they seem to yield to temptation again and again and again. They readily acknowledge, "The devil seems to get me there every time. Even though I know this is an area of weakness, I seem to be increasingly unable to resist a temptation in this area. I yield again and again, even though I don't really want to."

The devil knows you as well or better than you know yourself. If you know your area of weakness, believe me when I tell you that the devil knows that area of weakness too! He has used your repeated giving in to your weakness to create a stronghold in your mind.

A stronghold is a darkness in your thinking. A stronghold involves a recurring, compulsive thought pattern.

The devil often follows this pattern:

- You can have this.
- You should have this.
- You must have this.
- There's something wrong with you if you don't do your utmost to have this.
- Here's how you can have this.
- Now, go get this.

Bringing Our Thoughts into Submission to Christ

Reread what the apostle Paul wrote to the Corinthians: "The weapons of our warfare are not carnal but mighty in God for pulling down strongholds, *casting down arguments and every high thing that exalts itself against the knowledge of God,* bringing every thought into captivity to the obedience of Christ" (2 Cor. 10:4–5, italics added for emphasis).

Note the "arguments" and "every high thing."

"Arguments" refer to speculations —

false doctrines and false beliefs that sound like truth, but are not. They are what-if rationalizations and justifications — the thoughts that cause us to call into question whether God has said something, whether God has really forbidden something, or whether God really meant what He said. Arguments are rooted in debate, doubt, division, and deception.

"Every high thing" refers to lofty philosophies that sound wonderful, but are not productive or effective in building a person's relationship with God. We must stand against human arguments and philosophies if these arguments and philosophies are in any way opposed to the "knowledge of God" — in other words, if they are contrary to what the Bible commands or to the nature of God as He has revealed Himself to us in prayer and in study of Scripture. We have "every high thing" at work in us if we believe our ideas and beliefs supersede the commands of God.

Paul further wrote that we are to bring every thought "into captivity to the obedience of Christ." We are to control our thoughts rather than have our thoughts control us. It's up to each one of us to take captive and cast out any speculation, rationalization, justification, idea, or philosophical notion that is contrary to God's Word and God's will.

You are the one responsible for bringing your thought life into subjection to Christ Jesus — to His commands, His teachings, His character. God's Word challenges you to line up your thought life with God's thoughts so that you think as Christ thought, feel as Christ felt, and then live as Christ lived. The devil knows exactly how to get you to think the wrong things so that you will do the wrong things. The devil also knows what Christ thought, felt, and did. His goal, therefore, is to get you to think and feel in a way that is different from what Christ thought and felt.

Have you ever heard someone say, "Oh, his imagination is just running away with him," or "She got carried away by that notion"? These sayings refer to a person's thoughts having control over the person instead of the person having control over his or her thoughts.

Can thoughts and daydreams do that? Absolutely. A person can get so caught up in what he thinks, fantasizes, becomes enamored by, or dreams up that he makes foolish decisions and choices, wastes incredible amounts of time and resources, and fails to do anything that is of eternal benefit to himself or others.

When a person is trapped by an idea, we often say he is "obsessed" with the idea. He is no longer free to make rational, sound, objective decisions. He is no longer free to think the thoughts of God. Obsessions are not only dangerous to a person's mental health — they are dangerous to a person's spiritual health. The vast majority of obsessions are not godly. Obsessions very often lead a person to think about and to pursue activities, relationships, and substances that are not according to God's principles or commandments.

Your Power over Your Thoughts

Do you have to entertain the devil's ideas? No.

Do you have to allow his ideas to lodge in your mind and dwell on them? No!

You cannot keep the devil from launching fiery ideas, beliefs, desires, and temptations at you. You cannot keep yourself totally immune or free from all impulses or perceptions that might trigger a sinful response. But you can clothe yourself with the full identity of Christ Jesus and arm yourself with faith, hope, and God's Word to thwart the devil's temptations. You can keep tempting thoughts from lodging in your mind. You can keep from acting on a temptation or entering into sin.

The challenge of God's Word is that you are to take control of your thoughts and bring them into captivity — to subject them to obedience, to bring them in line with what God's Word teaches you and Christ Jesus exemplifies for you.

"But," you may say, "I can't change the way I think."

Oh, yes, you can. The longer you entertain a negative thought about your neediness, the more difficult it may be for you to change the way you think. But you can change the way you think. You can say, "I will not think about this. I will think about something else. I choose right now to focus my mind on a different thought — one that is pleasing to God and beneficial to my life."

A person who has a stronghold in his life will have to make a concerted, intentional, difficult, and sometimes prolonged attempt to change the way he thinks or responds to life. There's a good reason for the term *stronghold* — a recurring, compulsive thought pattern has a strong hold on a person. A person who habitually thinks lustful thoughts, wrong thoughts about the nature of God, greedy thoughts, fearful thoughts, jealous thoughts, or other similar negative thoughts will have a difficult time breaking the habit of his thinking. Nevertheless, he can do it.

If you recognize that you have a stronghold in your life, cry out to God to deliver you and release you from it. Ask the Lord to forgive you for the hours you've wasted in compulsive, obsessive thinking and sinful behavior. Ask Him to free you from discouragement, despair, and depression. Ask Him to set you free from worry and anxiety.

If you trust Him to set you free, He'll do it!

When flaming arrows come into your mind, immediately ask, *What does God say?*

Then ask yourself, *Does this fit who I am in Christ Jesus?*

Know God's Word. Know who you are in Christ Jesus. Know who He is in you! Openly acknowledge and choose to live in the awareness that He is your Truth, your Righteousness, and your Peace. He is your Savior. He is the Author and Finisher of your faith and the Fulfillment of your hope. He is the One who is ever present with you, who gives you help in every situation.

Don't Miss the CMD

When the devil's arrows come our way, we have a CMD — a critical moment of decision. In that moment we have the greatest power to accept a thought or let it go right on by.

The devil approached Eve and asked, "Has God indeed said, 'You shall not eat of every tree of the garden'?" (Gen. 3:1). The devil hurled an arrow of doubt. He cast an air of suspicion over whether God actually said what God said. The devil positioned his question in a "lack" category. He focused on whether God said they should not eat of every tree rather than on what God actually said.

Let's recall exactly what God said to Adam: "Of every tree of the garden you may freely eat; but of the tree of the knowledge of good and evil you shall not eat, for in the day that you eat of it you shall surely die" (Gen. 2:16–17). God's focus was on the fact that they could eat freely of every tree but one. The devil's focus was on the fact that they could not eat of one particular tree. God focused on what Adam and Eve could do. The devil focused on what they were not to do. The difference is subtle, but important.

The moment that the devil's question hit Eve's mind, she had her CMD — her critical moment of decision. She should have said right then, "Yes, that's what God said." She never should have allowed the devil to get beyond that first comment.

Instead, Eve entered into a conversation with the devil and tried to justify what God said. In the process, she misquoted God to the devil. She said, "We may eat the fruit of the trees of the garden; but of the fruit of the tree which is in the midst of the garden, God has said, 'You shall not eat it, nor shall you touch it, lest you die' " (Gen. 3:2–3). God had not said anything about touching the fruit. Eve also failed to identify that the forbidden tree was the Tree of the Knowledge of Good and Evil. She simply identified it as the tree in the center of the Garden. She looked at the tree's position, not its quality or nature. So often we fail when we get our eyes on a person's position or on the position that we would like to have in an organization or in society rather than look at the person's character or the nature of the job as-

131

sociated with the title.

God did not say to Adam, "You can't eat of the tree because it's at the center of the Garden." God said, "You are not to eat of the tree because it is the Tree of the Knowledge of Good and Evil." God did not want Adam and Eve to know evil. He wanted them to know only what was good. Therefore, He was seeking to protect them, not deprive them.

Too many people in our world today say, "You need to have certain experiences so you won't be naïve . . . you won't be innocent . . . you won't be gullible. You want to be sophisticated and savvy, don't you? You need to try this, have this, own this, or experience this if you're going to be knowledgeable and fit in to this society and culture."

What a lie that is! There's no sin in being naïve, innocent, or gullible. There's no glory in being sophisticated or savvy. There's no place in God's Word where He tells us that we must do our utmost to be knowledgeable and fit in to the greater society and culture. The exact opposite is true. God calls us to be innocent. He calls us to live in purity. He calls us to have no association with or knowledge of evil. He calls us to be separate from a sinful society and culture, and to avoid walking on a broad road that leads to destruction. (See Matthew 7:13.)

If someone says to you, "You need to try this drug or this drink so you'll know what it's like," ask, "Why do I need to know what it's like?"

How will trying something that is harmful to your body or mind help you relate to other people? The truth is, alcohol and drugs destroy relationships. The knowledge of what it's like to be drunk or high is useless, empty knowledge. You're better off not knowing!

The devil responded to Eve by saying, "You will not surely die. For God knows that in the day you eat of it your eyes will be opened, and you will be like God, knowing good and evil" (Gen. 3:4–5). What flaming arrow is being hurled? Another arrow of doubt — this time not only about what God said, but also about the goodness of God. The devil introduced to Eve the concept that God was holding out on her, He was denying her something that was good for her, and He was keeping her from achieving her full potential as a human being.

Eve missed a second CMD. She should have said, "That's a lie. God said we will

die, and God tells the truth all the time."
Instead, Eve kept listening. The devil said,
"God is withholding from you something
you would benefit from having!"

A toehold moved rapidly to becoming a
foothold!

Then the devil sent another rapid-fire
round of flaming missiles. He called attention to the beauty of the tree and its fruit.
He pointed to the "goodness" of the fruit
as food. He underscored the value of being
wise. He played to Eve's sense of beauty
and her high regard for wisdom. He appealed to her desire to be like God in every
way she could be. The Bible says, "So
when the woman saw that the tree was
good for food, that it was pleasant to the
eyes, and a tree desirable to make one
wise, she took of its fruit and ate" (Gen.
3:6). A foothold became a stronghold, and
the destruction was swift.

Let's look at another example in the
Bible. We read in 2 Samuel:

It happened in the spring of the year, at
the time when kings go out to battle,
that David sent Joab and his servants
with him, and all Israel; and they destroyed the people of Ammon and be-
sieged Rabbah. But David remained at

Jerusalem. Then it happened one evening that David arose from his bed and walked on the roof of the king's house. And from the roof he saw a woman bathing, and the woman was very beautiful to behold. So David sent and inquired about the woman. And someone said, "Is this not Bathsheba, the daughter of Eliam, the wife of Uriah the Hittite?" Then David sent messengers, and took her; and she came to him, and he lay with her, for she was cleansed from her impurity; and she returned to her house. (11:1–4)

David lived in a palace located at the highest residential point on Mount Zion. He could overlook the entire City of David — Jerusalem — from his balconies. One evening he arose and began to walk on the rooftop balconies of his palace. From that vantage point, he looked down and saw a woman bathing.

The moment he saw the woman, David had a CMD — a critical moment of decision. He should have turned his eyes and kept walking. David knew the law of God. He knew the heart of God and the principles of right and wrong. But David did not do what he knew to do. He paused to watch the woman and to watch her long enough to conclude that she was "very beautiful to behold."

A toehold was established, and it was about to become a foothold.

David sent for his advisors and inquired about the identity of the woman. He was already entertaining the idea of getting to know her and spending time with her.

David was told that she was the wife of a man named Uriah. That should have totally settled the issue. The woman was not available. She was married. David missed a second key CMD. He should have said, "Well, she's married. That settles it." But a foothold was about to become a stronghold.

David sent messengers to bring Bathsheba to him.

We don't know exactly how their relationship developed or how long it took between the time they met and the time they had sex together, but that was the outcome of their relationship. Bathsheba became pregnant as a consequence of their sexual sin.

David compounded the trouble he created. He ordered Uriah sent to the front lines of battle where he was sure to be killed. In effect, David authorized the death of Uriah. One sin led to the next.

Satan could not force David and he can't force you as a believer to think about something at length or to act on a fantasy or a wrong thought. You have the power to turn your eyes away, to walk away, to refuse to listen, to turn your attention to something else. You have the power to say no to a thought from the devil. You have the power to say no to sin.

Consider the sequence of thoughts or questions that must have come to David's mind, even for a few fleeting seconds:

Isn't this woman beautiful?

Who is this woman?

Why shouldn't I invite her over to the palace?

What's the harm in getting to know her, even if she is a married woman?

What's to keep me from having what I want?

Who's going to stop me from having sex with this beautiful woman whose husband is out of town?

What's to keep me from arranging her husband's death?

For each question, there was a godly answer or response, one that David knew in his mind and heart, but he refused to act upon. David could have said:

Yes, she's beautiful, but I have no business spying on her. I need to put my eyes in another direction.

I don't need to know who she is. I have a wife.

She has no place at the palace. Her place is in the home her husband has provided for her.

I have no business developing a relationship with a married woman.

To have sex with this woman is blatant adultery.

Even though this woman is pregnant with my child, it's wrong for me to have her loyal, brave husband killed.

David ignored every warning sign and sidestepped every wise response. Learn from his mistake.

Don't miss the CMD when the devil launches his fiery missiles into your heart and mind. Immediately act on God's truth and declare, "I will not entertain this idea. I will not fantasize about this. I will not dwell on this. I choose to think about something else." And then immediately turn to something that fully engages your mind — a project or conversation or thought that fits the description of Philippians 4:8: true, noble, just, pure, lovely, of good report, or praiseworthy!

To take captive every thought to Christ Jesus is to quench the fiery darts that the enemy launches into your mind.

To take captive every thought to Christ Jesus is to keep strongholds from developing.

To take captive every thought to Christ Jesus is to resist the devil and send him fleeing.

To take captive every thought of Christ Jesus is to turn your attention and your mental energies toward the things that truly are blessed, rewarding, and beneficial to you and to all of God's kingdom.

7

The Strategy Underlying Every Temptation

A friend recently shared with me her experience with one of her children many years ago. Her daughter was about two years old at the time. The family had gone for a Sunday afternoon walk in a nearby park, and they were about a block away from their home when suddenly their little girl sat down on the edge of the curb. They encouraged her to get up and keep walking, pointing out to her that their home was well within view.

She shook her head no.

"Get up," they encouraged her. "We're almost home."

"No," she said. "I can't walk any more steps."

"Sure you can," they said.

"No," she said again, "I'm too little."

That's the attitude a lot of people seem to have when it comes to facing temptation. They adopt an attitude of "I'm too

140

little," "I'm too weak," "I'm not able." Then they use that attitude to justify their yielding to temptation and committing a sin.

Feelings of weakness can be good or bad. If feelings of weakness drive a person to greater dependency upon God, the outcome is good! But if these feelings are allowed to spiral downward into sin or feelings of self-pity, discouragement, or despair, the results are obviously bad.

Do you remember the last time you faced a very strong, appealing temptation — something you wanted to do, something you wanted to possess, or something you did not want to do?

Did you walk away from the temptation?

Did you debate with yourself, attempting to rationalize what you should do, might do, or "could get away with"?

Did you give in to the temptation? Did you tell yourself later, "I'm not going to worry about that," or did you struggle with guilt?

Did you realize what was happening in that moment of strong temptation?

If you aren't aware of the strategy the devil uses in tempting you, you likely will keep struggling with temptations. You are likely to become entrapped in a cycle of defeat, which includes a loss of self-worth and the development of a victim mind-set.

If you aren't aware of what is happening to you when you are tempted and yield repeatedly to temptation, you will find yourself doing again and again the very things that you don't want to do but can't seem to keep from doing.

Temptation or Trial?

People sometimes confuse the terms *trial* and *temptation*. We must know the difference if we truly are going to be able to discern a temptation.

A trial is a time of testing with a goal of strengthening the person who is going through the trial. A trial reveals to a person an area of weakness so he can do something to strengthen himself or trust God in a deeper way to provide what is lacking. The trials God may send or allow in our lives are designed to test us and show us where we are weak and need to become stronger.

A temptation of the devil is intended to entice us to do evil. It is aimed at our eventual destruction.

A man once came to me and said,

"Pastor, I've lost my job. I've been trying to find a new job for eight weeks, but I'm not having any success. Do you think the devil caused me to lose my job? Is he tempting me, or is God trying me?"

I asked him, "How did you lose your job? Were you fired for something you did, or was your company going through hard times and needed to let some people go?"

He said, "I think it was a combination. The company was going through a reorganization after a merger, and I was one of the last people hired. If I did anything wrong, it was that I didn't do enough to show why I was more valuable than the other guys in my same position."

"I'm not sure promoting yourself would have made any difference," I said.

He thought for a few seconds and then said, "You're probably right."

"What kind of job are you looking for?" I asked him.

"Well, I was a first-line supervisor on an assembly line."

"Did you like that job?" I asked.

"It paid well," he said.

"That isn't what I asked," I said. "Did you like your job? Did you feel fulfilled in it? Did you really enjoy it? Did you look forward to Monday mornings?"

He hung his head. "No," he finally stated. "I really didn't enjoy that job."

"What would you like to do?" I asked.

"I'd really like to coach a softball team and teach physical education in a school. I have a teaching degree, and I love sports."

I said, "Sir, you weren't being attacked by the devil when you lost your job. You were being liberated by God!"

"What do you mean?"

"You are seeing this job loss as an attack from the devil because you're without work and without income right now. I see this as a time of trial in your life — God is revealing that you have been in the wrong line of work, given the talents and desires He has built into you. God is trying to get you to see that you need to be applying for jobs in schools, and until one of those jobs shows up, you need to be substitute teaching, helping out with a softball team, or doing something to put yourself into position to be hired as a teacher!" I didn't have to say any more.

This man's face lit up as if I had turned a light onto him. He had enthusiasm in his eyes. "That's it," he said. "I've been thinking the devil stole my job. The truth is that God wants me to have a better job! It may not be better in pay, but it sure would be better for me."

"God can show you how to live with a little less money," I assured him. "And here's one thing I've seen happen again and again. When people work in a job they love, financial opportunities come their way. God provides."

This man clearly was experiencing a trial from God — a trial intended to move him into the job that God desired for him to have.

The Nature of a Temptation

A temptation is an enticement by the devil that always includes sin and is always aimed at destroying us in some way. A temptation can occur through the devil speaking directly to our minds and hearts, or by the devil speaking through a human being who is functioning under the devil's influence. The temptation is aimed at getting us to use our God-given gifts to gratify God-given desires and drives in an ungodly, wrong way at the wrong time. Every phrase of this definition is important for you to consider.

Temptations Come from the Devil

God does not tempt us. Never. God's Word declares that God "does not afflict willingly, nor grieve the children of men" (Lam. 3:33).

Satan is the tempter. He has access to our minds and hearts to plant impulses and ideas. Sometimes he speaks directly. Sometimes he speaks through a human being who is used by the devil to deliver his message to us. That human being may not be possessed by the devil. The human being may be functioning in the flesh in a careless, thoughtless way — not even knowing that what he is saying to us is part of the enemy's plot against us. Oftentimes the devil will plant an ungodly idea in a person's mind, not to entice him to commit sin, but to get him to express the idea to someone else.

How do we know this is true? Because Jesus warned against this very practice. On one occasion His disciples asked Him, "Who is the greatest in the kingdom of heaven?" Jesus called a little child to Him and set the child in the midst of them. Then Jesus said, "Unless you are converted and become as little children, you will by no means enter the kingdom of heaven." He went on to say, "Whoever receives one little child like this in My name receives Me. But whoever causes one of these little ones who believe in Me to sin, it would be better for him if a millstone were hung around his neck, and he were drowned in the depth of the sea. Woe to the world because of offenses! For offenses must come, but woe to that man by whom the offense comes!" (See Matthew 18:1–7.)

Jesus was referring not only to children in the physical realm, but also to those who are young in their faith. He stated that people — men as well as women — can function as agents of offense. In other words, they can cause a weaker person to stumble and sin. Jesus spoke to those who are agents of offense in very strong terms, "Woe to that person!" Jesus pointed out that offenses come — we can't stop all temptations and hurts — but Jesus made it very clear that we must never intentionally or unintentionally tempt, hurt, or cause others to be tripped up in their faith.

Temptations May Be Aimed at Our God-Given Gifts

The devil comes to you at a time of neediness — emotional, physical, spiritual

— but his temptation is aimed at one of your strengths. For example, the devil might come to a gifted preacher at a time when that preacher is feeling a need to receive greater recognition and appreciation. The devil does not come with the lie, "You really aren't much of a preacher." No! He usually comes with the lie, "You should be preaching more. You should be speaking to much bigger crowds. You should be speaking more often — people really need your sermons."

As another example, the devil might come to a woman who is seeking to do everything in her power to be the best wife, mother, and homemaker she can be. The devil comes at a time when that woman is feeling underappreciated and perhaps even unloved. He doesn't say to her, "You aren't much of a homemaker." No! He usually comes with the lie, "Your husband should be complimenting you more and doing nicer things for you. He doesn't deserve you. You are way too fine a woman for him."

Temptations May Address God-Given Desires and Drives

There's nothing wrong with having a desire to be appreciated, loved, valued, recognized, rewarded, or treated in an honorable, respectful way. There's nothing wrong with having physical needs and sexual desires. There's nothing wrong with having a strong ambition to do your best and to find real meaning and purpose in life. There's nothing wrong with a desire to use your talents and work hard. God built all of these desires and drives into you as a human being. The devil never comes to deny your desires and drives — he comes to reinforce the truth that you have these desires and drives.

Temptations Are Enticements to Meet God-Given Desires and Drives in an Ungodly or Wrong Way

The devil will say to the underappreciated, gifted preacher, "You need to promote yourself more — you need to call attention to the fact that you are a better preacher than a certain person who seems to have more pulpit time than you have." The devil won't use the words *gossip, undermine, destroy the reputation of,* or *spread rumors about* because that language would be too obvious. He'll entice the gifted preacher to "speak up for yourself" and to "tell the truth about your desire to preach more" and "point out to others the ways in which you are a successful preacher — in fact, the most successful preacher in this church or in this city."

The devil will say to the undervalued wife, "You know, there are men who would certainly appreciate you more than your husband appreciates you. In fact . . ."

Now, the devil may not plant this idea in the wife's mind. He may just bring someone into her life who begins to compliment her, appreciate her, value her, and point out her many wonderful qualities.

The devil's lie is always, "You need this. You deserve it. You should take steps to have what you need and deserve."

At times, the devil will hold out to you what you need or deserve, but entice you to get ahead of God or to drag your feet when it comes to timing. Many people find that once they know what God desires for them, they move very quickly to attain what they know God has for them. They don't wait for God's perfect timing. They rush into a relationship, they throw themselves completely into an effort to get what they desire with an attitude of "I have to make this happen!" or they pull out all stops in their pursuit of a goal without any regard to how their actions affect other people who might be involved in the accomplishment of that goal. Other people know what God desires for them, but they are fearful or distrustful and they stall in acting quickly when God speaks to them.

God not only has a perfect way to meet the needs and desires He has built into each one of us, but He has perfect timing for meeting those needs and desires. If the devil can't trip us up to pursue the wrong goals, he certainly will try to get us to make an error when it comes to timing — enticing us to rush ahead or to lag behind.

Temptations Come to Everyone

Nobody is beyond temptation. Nobody is immune to it or shielded from it. Nobody can live a life without facing temptation.

No matter how devoted a person may be to Jesus Christ, Satan can slip up on his blind side and tempt him in a way that is not only surprising, but alluring and deadly.

Adam and Eve were in the Garden of Eden at the time the devil tempted them. They were in a perfect environment, and they were absolutely sinless initially. Yet when they were tempted, they yielded to that temptation! No environment and no degree of purity can keep you from being tempted. Don't expect it.

The Devil Has a Strategy

The devil has a specific strategy. He doesn't operate in a haphazard way. He has used his strategy from the beginning of time. Why? Because it works! We human beings keep falling for the same strategy generation after generation.

Satan's foremost strategy is revealed in his temptations of Adam and Eve in the Garden of Eden. He revealed to them just how subtle he can be in his manipulation and temptation, and also how devastating the consequences can be when a human being gives in to his temptations.

Throughout the Old Testament, Satan used the same tactics and measures again and again. In the New Testament, he used the same kinds of deceptions, lies, and manipulations. Why should he change strategy? It has worked for thousands of years.

If we're honest, we have to admit that his strategy works on us, unless we are aware of it and armed against it. His strategy begins with need.

Strategic Move #1:
A Focus on Needs

Satan directs us to a specific need or desire in our lives. This desire in your life may not be at all the desire in the life of your spouse, a friend, a sibling, or an associate at work. Each of us has a unique set of needs and desires, and some needs and desires are stronger than others. The devil focuses on our strongest need and desire.

Some people question, "Is the devil omniscient — does he know all things about me?" No, his knowledge is limited.

"Then how," a person may ask, "does the devil know my needs and desires?" He observes the way you live! In observing your life, he can see where you are weak by the choices you make, the things to which you gravitate, and the things you habitually show an interest in or express an interest in doing.

The devil will lie to you in two ways about the needs in your life.

First, the devil tells you that you have a need that God can't meet. The implication is always, "God is holding out on you. He is failing to give you something. He has something that you need, and He isn't providing it." Adam and Eve didn't need anything in the Garden of Eden. All of their needs were met fully. Even in that situation, the devil offered his lie: you need something more in your life, and God is withholding it from you.

Second, the devil tells you that he is capable of meeting your need. Now, the devil never claims that he can meet your need fully for the rest of your life without any negative consequences. He doesn't tell you the full truth about his capability to meet your need.

Rather, he holds out evidence that he can meet the need.

You need more excitement? Here, try this.

You have a physical need to be met? Here, this is for you.

You need to feel more important? Here, this'll do it.

The devil told Eve the risk of eating the fruit of the knowledge of good and evil was minimal: "You will not surely die." He held out for her only what seemed to be the good aspect of her partaking of the Tree of the Knowledge of Good and Evil: "Your eyes will be opened, and you will be like God, knowing good and evil."

The devil didn't tell Eve that she would destroy her relationship with God or her relationship with Adam, or lose her place in Eden.

The devil won't tell you the full consequences of the sin he entices you to commit.

He won't tell you what adultery will do to your marriage, your relationship with your children, or your reputation.

He won't remind you that alcohol leads to liver disease, nicotine leads to lung cancer, or obesity leads to heart problems.

He won't caution you that sex can lead to an unwanted pregnancy, or that an abortion will scar you for life, perhaps physically and, most assuredly, emotionally.

He won't warn you that getting high on drugs can lead to accidental death or brain dysfunction.

The devil never tells the full consequences of any sin — he holds out only the immediate self-gratification.

Questions to Ask About Your Neediness

You must always ask vital questions about your needs, especially the area of need in your life that the devil repeatedly seems to attack:

What is the real need in my life? What

need is the devil playing on?

Every person has four basic physical needs: food, water, air, and physical security.

Every person has four basic emotional needs: human love and acceptance, feelings of competency, praise or recognition that lead to feelings of worthiness, and purpose or usefulness.

Every person has four basic spiritual needs: God's unconditional love, God's forgiveness of sins, the assurance of everlasting life, and an awareness of God's abiding presence that gives hope for the future and confidence that God is always in control.

Can God meet all of your physical needs? Absolutely. The Bible has dozens of stories and references that point to God's ability and desire to meet your physical needs. He provided manna, and water from a rock for the Israelites. He provided safety in the face of all kinds of danger. And what He did for the people of the Bible, He does today for His people.

Can God meet your spiritual needs? Absolutely. Jesus said, "For God so loved the world that He gave His only begotten Son, that whoever believes in Him should not perish but have everlasting life. For God did not send His Son into the world to condemn the world, but that the world through Him might be saved" (John 3:16–17). God so loved. God forgives the sins of and gives eternal life to those who believe in Jesus Christ and receive Him as their Savior. God has a future for you, and it is a good one. Read God's assurance in Jeremiah 29:11: "I know the thoughts that I think toward you, says the LORD, thoughts of peace and not of evil, to give you a future and a hope." The apostle Paul wrote, "And now abide faith, hope, love, these three" (1 Cor. 13:13). Faith, hope, and love are the three great spiritual gifts of God.

Can God meet your emotional needs? Absolutely. But it is on this point that people are most often tripped up. They don't trust God for love and acceptance. They don't believe God will help them discover their gifts and become competent in using them. They don't feel worthy — perhaps because they have been told repeatedly that they are unworthy, or because they feel that their sins put them beyond the realm of worthiness in God's eyes. They don't feel as if they have a purpose for living; therefore, they don't live a life of purpose and fail to feel satisfied and fulfilled.

The truth, however, is that God can meet all of your emotional needs. He does this directly through the abiding presence of the Holy Spirit in your life. He also does this by sending people into your life who can wrap their arms around you and love you, encourage you, build you up, applaud you, and help you discover your unique gifts and ways in which to use them for the greatest good — now and in eternity.

Let me ask you . . .

What will an experience rooted in sin really do to help you feel love and acceptance? Will an act of physical sex give that feeling? No. Someone may believe that having sexual intimacy with a person will produce love, but the morning after, he awakens to the stark realization that it does not produce love — very often, it produces disdain or rejection.

Will taking a drug give a feeling of competency? The person high on drugs may feel as if he were better than ever, but in truth, his physical and mental reactions are impaired and the low after the high always negates any good done during the high.

Will stealing a valuable object provide a feeling of worthiness? A person may be able to show off a possession to the admiration of a few peers, but there's nothing enviable about a jail sentence for grand theft or burglary.

Will cheating to win an award provide recognition? Perhaps for a few moments, but when the cheating is discovered, the infamy will produce a kind of recognition the cheater never desired!

When you are tempted, ask yourself: *What need in my life does the devil seem to be addressing? Why do I have this need? What have I done to allow this need to develop?*

Why don't I believe God can meet that need? Why do I believe the devil can?

Reconsider your understanding about who God is and what God is capable of doing. I encourage you to focus on the attributes of God and the names of God as they are revealed in Scripture. God is our Rock, our firm Foundation, our Mighty Fortress. He is our Savior, Deliverer, Healer, Redeemer, and the One who makes us whole. God is our Helper, our Comforter, our Counselor, our Father who gives good gifts to His children. If you don't believe God is able to meet your needs, you aren't seeing God in the fullness of who He is!

Reconsider your relationship with God. If you do not believe God is willing to meet your needs, ask yourself why you don't believe He will. Have you bought into one of the most basic of the devil's lies that God doesn't love you, won't forgive you, or doesn't really care what happens to you? God's Word says otherwise! God's Word says He loves you unconditionally and without measure — so much so that He sent Jesus to the cross to die for your sins.

If you don't believe God will forgive you because your sins are too great or too entrenched, read again 1 John 1:9: "If we confess our sins, He is faithful and just to forgive us our sins and to cleanse us from all unrighteousness." If you don't believe God cares what happens to you, reread the words of Jesus in the gospel of John, chapters 14 through 17. Jesus repeatedly told His disciples that He would be with them and abide with them, and that they would be in Him and be comforted by the Holy Spirit in their lives.

God is more than willing to meet all of your needs. Check out your beliefs about God and your relationship with Him. Ask yourself why you don't want to believe God's Word.

Strategic Move #2: An Ungodly Means to a Godly End

Satan comes to you at your moment of greatest need with an urgent message that you can and should use an ungodly method or means to achieve a godly result. Satan's temptations always have a sense of urgency about them. That urgency exists because you have allowed a need to grow in you.

At times the devil keeps the pressure on so that a need seems desperate. The temptation is fired again and again, and with such intensity that you begin to doubt, *Will God really meet this need?* The answer to the question is always yes. Don't lose sight of the answer. The devil will cause the question to loom so large it may seem to fill your mind day and night. You may begin to lose sight of the answer. The answer is always, "Yes, God will meet this need. He will do it in His way, in His timing, and He will do it in a way that is entirely for my eternal good without any negative consequences!"

Psychologists for years have advocated that people HALT. They know that if a person gets too hungry (H), too angry (A), too lonely (L), or too tired (T), he is in danger of emotional imbalance or continued depression. Before these negative situations can arise, make sure that you meet these physical and emotional needs to the best of your ability.

Take care of your physical body — eat and drink what is healthful. Get sufficient rest and relaxation. Work and spend your physical resources wisely to provide for yourself the adequate shelter and clothing you need. Choose what is pure — the cleanest water, whole foods, and clean air.

Take care of your soul — your mind and emotions. Make friends and sustain those friendships. Nurture your marriage and your relationship with your children. If you aren't married and don't have children, find some children to whom you can be a mentor, teacher, or older, caring adult. At the same time, find someone who can mentor, teach, or care for you, someone who can help you become all God created you to be, someone who will encourage you always to develop and use your talents fully, and someone who will motivate you to give yourself away to people in need. Choose to feed into your soul what is most beneficial. Paul gave this word of wise advice to the Philippians:

Whatever things are true, whatever things are noble, whatever things are just, whatever things are pure, whatever things are lovely, whatever things are of good report, if there is any virtue and if there is anything praiseworthy — meditate on these things. (Phil. 4:8)

As you choose the movies you will watch and television programs you will see, the music and tapes you will listen to, the books and magazines you will read, the places you will go, the topics of conversation in which you will engage, the friendships you seek to cultivate, consider the criteria in Philippians 4:8.

If you are intent upon establishing godly relationships, taking into your thought life and emotions the experiences and ideas that will nurture your soul, and avail yourself of the best mentors and teachers, you can avoid giving the devil a toehold of emotional need.

Take care of your spirit. If you need to confess your sin, do so. Receive God's forgiveness. If you aren't experiencing all of God's love, presence, and power in your life that you would like to experience, re-evaluate your spiritual disciplines. Spend more time reading and studying your

163

Bible. Spend more time in praise and in prayer. Get more involved with other believers in your church — perhaps in a small group study or in an outreach ministry. Above all, ask the Holy Spirit to help you daily to live out your faith in a positive, steady manner.

Ends Don't Justify Means

Notice that I also stated that the devil's temptation nearly always presents an ungodly method or means to achieve a godly result. The devil will tell you repeatedly: "The end will justify any means."

The truth of God is that the means are just as important as the end results and goals. Ungodly methods and means are never to be employed, no matter how godly the goal may be.

Suppose someone asked me today, "Don't you want to be more like God? Don't you want to understand God's Word as much as you can so you can truly have the mind of Christ?" My answer to both questions would be, "Yes!" I want to be more godly in all my thoughts, feelings, attitudes, opinions, and behaviors. I want to have more and more insight into God's Word so I truly can think the way Jesus thought and respond to life the way Jesus responded to it.

The trick of the devil, however, is to offer us an ungodly means of getting to a godly goal.

Is it wrong for a person to want to have his sexual needs met? No. Is it wrong to commit fornication or adultery in order to meet those needs? Yes.

Is it wrong for a person to want to eat because he is hungry? No. Is it wrong to eat like a glutton without any regard to whether other people at the table have enough to eat? Yes.

Is it wrong for a person to want to feel at peace? No. Is it wrong to take illegal drugs to induce temporary feelings of peace that ultimately leave the person more anxious and drug dependent than before? Yes.

When the Holy Spirit led Jesus into the wilderness, He fasted forty days and forty nights. The Bible tells us, "And in those days He ate nothing, and afterward, when they had ended, He was hungry" (Luke 4:2). In that state of great physical hunger, the devil came to Jesus with the temptation, "If You are the Son of God, command this stone to become bread" (Luke 4:3).

Was it wrong for Jesus to be hungry or to seek to find bread to eat after forty days of fasting and praying? No. Was it wrong for Jesus to misuse His spiritual power to turn stones into bread? Yes.

The devil came to Jesus at precisely the point of Jesus' immediate need and attempted to persuade Him to meet that need but in an ungodly, inappropriate way.

The devil does the same thing in our lives. He comes at us with a legitimate need or desire and suggests that we meet our need in a way that is contrary to God's commandments.

The devil desires for us to satisfy ourselves and, in so doing, to get off course from God's plan for our lives.

Strategic Move #3: An Urgent Opportunity

Satan presents an opportunity for you to meet your need now. He will present an appealing opportunity — it will appear to more than meet your immediate need with the greatest amount of sensory pleasure or material gain! But the opportunity will also appear to be fleeting. It will be presented as an opportunity that you need to seize immediately.

It is no coincidence that when you feel the greatest physical need for sex, the devil brings across your path a person who is very appealing and very available.

It is no coincidence that when you feel the poorest — not only in the amount of money you have but in your self-esteem — the devil brings across your path an opportunity for a get-rich or you-can-have-it-all-right-now scheme.

It is no coincidence that when you feel the hungriest, he brings across your path a commercial or billboard for the most appealing food items.

The devil wants you to act immediately before you have any time to think through your decision!

The questions you must always ask are these: What are the full consequences of my pursuing this path of sin? Am I willing to pay the price of those consequences if they take their full course? Is this really the path that will result in my happiness, peace, and success?

I was discussing these questions with someone not long ago, and the person said to me in a half-teasing way, "You don't need to preach to me, Preacher. I know what's right to do." I believe most people could make that statement.

We know how to behave, what to eat, how to exercise, what to avoid, what to do, and how to respond. We know what to do!

When we are tempted, we need to pause, take a deep breath, and reflect for a few moments on what we know is the right way to live.

Take the time to ask yourself some very basic questions. You know the answers!

- Is all sexual immorality against God's Word? Are adultery, fornication, and homosexual and lesbian behavior wrong according to the Bible?
- What have been the consequences in the lives of other people who have yielded to this sin?
- If I yield, how will this affect me? What impact will it have on me emotionally? How will it affect God's plan for my life? How will it affect people around me — especially my family members and friends who love me? How will it affect my future?
- Am I willing to pay the consequences of yielding?
- Will yielding to this temptation satisfy me or stir up an even stronger desire? Does a little drug use usually create a desire for more drug use? Does a little gambling usually create a desire to gamble more?
- Is yielding to this temptation a wise

decision or a foolish one?

- How can I do this against the God who loves me so much? The compelling question asked by Joseph when he was tempted by Potiphar's wife is a question we are always wise to ask: "How then can I do this great wickedness, and sin against God?" (Gen. 39:9).

The devil nearly always couches his temptations in a sense of urgency: *You have to make this decision right now. You can't let this opportunity slip away. You need to have this immediately. You really, really, really need this. You shouldn't fail to get this now.*

The truth is, we nearly always can wait for minutes, hours, even days before we make a decision related to sin. The devil knows that if we wait until the moment of passion passes, the object is out of sight, and the emotional heat is replaced with a rational cool head, we will not be nearly as prone to give in to his temptation.

When you are tempted . . . pause. Wait. Think. Reflect on what you know to do that is right before God.

An Example of the Strategy in Operation

Let me remind you again how the devil dealt with Eve in the Garden of Eden.

In all likelihood, Eve was already looking at the fruit when the devil came to her. She was probably hungry. She might have been tired of working to pick fruits and vegetables for dinner. She might have been frustrated that she had been looking for ripe fruit all day and hadn't yet come across any. She likely was already wondering what it would be like to taste and touch that forbidden fruit. She was already questioning why God would keep it off-limits to her. She was within reach of it when the devil came to her. He merely played on what he could already see was the desire in her own eyes and heart.

The devil certainly didn't want Eve to leave the moment in which her desire for the forbidden fruit was strongest. He wanted to keep her on the line, keep her engaged in the conversation, keep her questioning and wondering until she gave in. He wanted to keep her in a heightened state of neediness.

Satan asked Eve, "Has God indeed said, 'You shall not eat of every tree of the garden'?" And Eve replied, "We may eat the fruit of the trees of the garden; but of the fruit of the tree which is in the midst of the garden, God has said, 'You shall not eat it, nor shall you touch it, lest you die.' "

Then the serpent said to Eve, "You will not surely die. For God knows that in the day you eat of it your eyes will be opened, and you will be like God, knowing good and evil."

Now look at what Eve did! The Bible tells us that when Eve "saw that the tree was good for food, that it was pleasant to the eyes, and a tree desirable to make one wise, she took of its fruit and ate." (See Genesis 3:1–6.)

What were the three great needs in Eve's life? They are identified for us:

1. She had a physical desire for what tasted good and satisfied her hunger.
2. She had a desire for beauty.
3. She had a desire for knowledge to be more like God.

These three desires are present to some degree in virtually every person:

1. Physical drives and pleasures. Every person has a desire for pleasure — for what seems to be good and satisfying in meeting physical needs and drives. Each of us has a desire for food, but also a hunger for many other things — for love, for sex, for things that make us feel good.

2. *Beauty.* Every person has a desire for things that seem lovely. Certainly not every person has the same taste or style — what is good looking to one person may not be at all appealing to another person. We want to own or possess what is beautiful to us. We want other people to admire us because of the beauty we have been able to create, acquire, or portray.

3. *Knowledge.* Every person has a desire to learn. Learning is a great natural high. Just look at a toddler's joy in exploring every facet of his world. We derive tremendous satisfaction from having new insights and gaining new levels of understanding. Every person I've ever known is interested in finding out secrets, discovering more about how certain things work, understanding himself better, and gaining insight into what makes other people tick.

When knowledge is presented to us in a way that we believe gives us power, that knowledge can become even more desirable! We want insider information, and not just about how to invest our money. We want to be "in the know" so we can exert influence and authority. In other words, we want to be "more like God," as the serpent tempted Eve.

The devil tells us that we deserve to have our needs met. We deserve to have the most beautiful, the best, the most pleasing. We deserve to have access to information and to develop our minds. We deserve these things because we deserve to develop our potential and fulfill our destiny.

Many people ultimately define success as having all of their needs met, surrounding themselves with the most beautiful objects that can be purchased — from lovely homes to fancy cars to beautiful clothes and jewelry — and having the best education and training available.

Anticipating and Avoiding Satan's Temptations

How might you anticipate and then avoid putting yourself into a position where you are likely to experience temptation?

You need to address two main areas of your life.

1. Your Current Need and Need Level

What is the main need in your life right now? How intensely are you feeling that need? Is there a habit or addiction that has you in its grip?

Satan knows your area of weakness or need, as well as your level of need, and that is where he will tempt you. Do you have a need for justice? A need for appreciation or recognition? A need for love? A need for reward? A physical need?

Consider for a moment a person who believes he is being punished unfairly for something he did not do. The more he dwells on the injustice he is feeling, the more he feels compelled to do something about the injustice. The more he dwells on what he might do, the closer he comes to taking action on the idea — he begins to plot and plan ways in which he might take justice into his own hands.

Behind all of this is the deception that God is incapable of dealing with the injustice, or that God doesn't care that an injustice has occurred. The person falsely concludes, "God doesn't love me. God doesn't care about this pain I'm feeling. God isn't going to do anything to give me the justice I deserve. I need to take care of this myself."

Why do people suddenly seem to go berserk and kill innocent people, lash out in ways that seem extreme or over the top, or speak with such anger and hatred that it seems as if a volcano inside them has suddenly erupted? Because they have been dwelling on an unmet need in their lives, and rather than trust God to meet that need, they have been stewing in their pain and brewing up ways in which they might handle the pain of their injustice in their own power.

Consider for a moment a person who believes that she isn't appreciated. Nobody seems to acknowledge her, reward her, or value who she is or what she does. She begins to think back over her life and concludes that she has never been appreciated — her parents didn't appreciate her; her siblings didn't appreciate her; her teachers didn't appreciate her. The thoughts and impressions from the past come at a faster and faster pace. Finally she concludes that she has always been put down by other people and that nobody has ever valued her. She says to herself, *I need to go out and make my own mark on the world. I need to be free of all restraints so I can truly express myself and win the approval of people who will finally see me for the person I am. I need to do something that will spell achievement to other people, and with my achievement will come appreciation.* So, she leaves her husband and family, goes out to make her mark on the world, and then can't understand why all of her efforts seem to fail. She never takes responsibility for her failures. She continues to blame others for failing to recognize her talents, abilities, and worthiness.

What has happened? She has allowed her mind to dwell on an unmet need in her life, and she has refused to turn to God who alone can give her the sense of value and worthiness that she craves. She seeks to meet her unmet need in her own power, according to her own devices and methods.

Consider the man who concludes that his wife is no longer willing to meet his sexual needs or to understand all the pressures he is under in his career. He equates the two, saying to himself, *If she cared about the pressures I'm facing, she would want to comfort me in a way that would allow me to feel release from the stress.* He begins to dwell more and more on the ways in which he feels deprived of his wife's love and affection. The more he dwells on his need, the more he notices

176

that women other than his wife seem to have regard for him. They seem to be concerned about him, tender toward him, and loving in what they say and do. He begins to reach out to a woman other than his wife in hopes that his need will be met. He ends up in an affair, and in the months that follow, he loses not only his lover, but also his wife and family.

What happened in his life? He allowed his mind to dwell on what he perceived to be an unmet need. He refused to turn to God with that need, trusting God to speak to the heart of his wife or to show him ways to communicate better with his wife. He began to seek a way to meet his need in his own power, according to his own devices and methods.

In each case, the thought pattern leads the person to rely on self more than on God. A growing, increasingly strong, and increasingly negative or sinful thought pattern compels the person to act on his thoughts. The actions that are rooted in self-centered need-meeting cause the person to take actions that hurt others and ultimately to experience consequences that are far more painful than the initial need the person felt.

What is your need level? The greater the

feelings of need in your life, the more vulnerable you are.

Level of need and level of success can be related. In some cases, a person's need level is directly related to his success level!

The more effective you are, the more successful you are, the more famous you are, the holier you are, the more the devil will try to tempt you to make a mistake that will destroy your reputation, your integrity, and your witness for Christ. People seem to think that if a person rises to a certain level of spiritual maturity, that person will become immune to temptation. Not so! Never forget that the devil came at Jesus, the Son of God, with intense temptation! And he did so on more than one occasion.

What can you do?

First, identify the environments and times in which you feel the most vulnerable.

Second, take action to change those environments and to eliminate those vulnerable times.

If you find that you overspend your budget on frivolous purchases and you feel guilty and ashamed of yourself as a result — feeling that you haven't been a good steward of God's resources entrusted to you — ask yourself when you go on shopping sprees. Is it when you are feeling particularly low on self-esteem or self-worth? Is it after someone has rejected you or criticized you at work or at home or perhaps in another setting? When you feel as if somebody has put you down, do you immediately go to the mall and shop?

Choose to do something other than shop in those moments of weakness and temptation. Go for a walk around the block instead.

If you find yourself routinely overeating to the detriment of your health, ask yourself when you overeat and what triggers those overeating binges. Is it when you allow yourself to get too hungry? Is it when you are feeling lonely? Do you come home from work exhausted, too hungry to cook a proper meal? Do you plop down in front of a television set that gives you commercial after commercial for food products and order a pizza and eat the entire pizza while watching programs that give you a false sense of connection with society?

Choose to do something other than eat in those moments of weakness. Go to the gym and work out instead!

2. Your General "Bent" Toward Sin

In addition to monitoring your need and your need level, you should gain an understanding of your general bent toward sin.

Every person seems to have a propensity or bent toward a particular sin or sins. Three big categories of sin are described in 1 John 2:16: "For all that is in the world — the lust of the flesh, the lust of the eyes, and the pride of life — is not of the Father but is of the world."

To lust is to crave, to have an intense and insatiable desire for. Some people have a lust of the flesh — they want what satisfies physical cravings and desires. The lust of the flesh can be an insatiable desire for sex. It can also be an insatiable desire for a chemical substance that impacts the flesh, creating a feeling of intense excitement, expansion, energy, or relaxation. The lust of the flesh generally refers to anything that someone uses to satisfy desires of the flesh.

The lust of the eyes refers to things that we see and just have to have. The lust of the eyes often manifests itself in covetousness, jealousy, and greed. Generally speaking, the lust of the eyes refers to a person's desire for things — for material possessions and objects perceived to have value.

The pride of life refers to things that satisfy a person's inner longing for value or esteem. A person who has the pride of life craves awards, fame, rewards, applause, and outward expressions of appreciation more than anything else, including time with family. He often pursues political office, the arts, or advanced degrees solely to achieve a level of respectability or recognition he desires. Generally speaking, the pride of life refers to anything that a person seeks as a means of meeting an insatiable inner drive for love and worthiness.

From time to time, we all are prone to each of these broad categories of sin, but in many people, there's a focused desire in one of these areas. What do you find you most need? Where do you often feel a lack or a dissatisfaction in your life?

The enemy, of course, knows your nature. He knows your propensity for sin. He knows your lusts and pride. How does he know? By watching what you choose and what you seek out. By watching your past behavior. By watching where you have fallen into sin in the past.

Certainly God has given to each of us an ability to enjoy things physically, sensually, sexually. We have been given senses so we can enjoy the sight, smell, taste, touch, and sounds of His creation. God has also given us an ability to appreciate beauty. He has given us an ability to learn, grow, exercise wisdom, and love and be loved. It is not wrong for any person to enjoy life, to have nice things, and to develop himself within the guidelines God has established.

Satan entices us to go beyond the boundaries that God has established. Satan attempts to get us to ignore God's commandments and make up our own rules for how much we should have when it comes to physical, emotional, and material satisfaction. The devil wants us to seek to be the God of our own lives rather than worship the almighty Lord God. The devil knows that in worshiping ourselves, we are actually doing his bidding. We are breaking off our ability to experience God's love, mercy, and forgiveness. We are substituting our will for His will, and when that happens, we are saying no to a deeper relationship with God.

Never Lose Sight of the End Game

Never forget the devil's purposes:

- To draw you away from God
- To thwart God's purpose for your life
- To deny the glory of God in your life
- To destroy you in any way he can, including physical health

Bear in mind always that the devil doesn't reveal his ultimate intent at the outset of any temptation. If he did, we'd never give in! He doesn't tell us or convince us of the full consequences he intends for us. No, he seeks only to get us to try what we want to try. His temptation to us is not, "I'd like to give you an addiction that can lead to lung cancer." His temptation is usually in the form of questions and subtle suggestions that play on what we already desire: "Doesn't that look good? Don't you wonder what it's like? You know you want to try it just once. Why not try it? You're old enough in spite of what anybody else may think or say. You know you'd like to have this experience so others won't call you a Goody Two-shoes." And on and on it goes. The devil puts all of his efforts on the initial yielding to his temptation.

The devil does his utmost to black out everything else except your need or desire. He doesn't want you looking at anything else or thinking about anything else. He wants 100 percent of your focus on your need and the fact that it isn't fully met.

The devil also does his utmost to keep you in the now moment of your need. He doesn't want you thinking about the past and the ways in which God may have met your need in the past. He doesn't want you thinking about the future and that your need may be met in a legitimate or godly way in the future. He wants you thinking about how to get your need met now, now, now. He tries to keep you in a state of urgency.

The devil's ultimate goal is to get you to sin. And sin separates you from God as well as from other people. Sin produces death — spiritually, emotionally, and physically.

8
Responding to Temptation

Is there one area of your life in which you seem to keep failing? Why do you think that is so?

Do you find yourself saying, "I don't know why I can't control this when everything else in my life seems to be under control"?

Why is this happening?

How are you responding?

Do you know what to do?

Do you feel angry, bitter, resentful, or hateful — acting in a way that you know is vindictive, manipulative, or revengeful? Are you willing to address the fact that these feelings may very well be related to a temptation that you are not responding to in a godly way?

There is a godly way to respond to temptation and to resist the strategy of the devil against your life. But first, you must honestly ask yourself, *Do I really want to resist the temptation?*

Many people waver when it comes to resisting temptations. They aren't quite sure they want to resist temptations — at least not all temptations, all the time, and in all circumstances. Many people want to be able to pick and choose the sin they fall into, generally because they think they can quickly erase any damage caused by that sin. They are wrong on two accounts.

In the first place, they can't select the sin they want to commit.

In the second place, they don't have the authority to erase the consequences or damage caused by the sin.

The power to resist temptations comes only as we make a decision to accept Jesus as Savior and make a firm commitment to follow Jesus as the Lord of our lives every day of our lives.

This commitment is renewable day by day by day.

It is a commitment that we are called by God to make with "steadfastness" and "faithfulness."

It is a commitment of the total self — spirit, mind, emotions, and body.

To make a commitment to Christ is to make a decision to do what Jesus commanded us to do and to pursue with the whole heart, mind, and soul, the pure, wholesome, godly, and holy life that He lived. Jesus commanded us to be "perfect" — which means to be whole. He commanded us to love one another. He commanded us to be diligent in keeping His teachings. He commanded us to be His witnesses at all times in all places. He commanded us to walk boldly by faith and to trust God to meet our needs, regardless of what those needs might be. Jesus gave all of Himself to us, and in return, Jesus requires all of us. That's what it means to take up our cross daily and follow Him. That's what it means to truly "walk the walk" and not just "talk the talk" of being a Christian.

Included in our total commitment to Christ are a total desire and a commitment not to sin. Our pursuit is for righteousness — the things that are pleasing to God. Our desire is to run from sin, to withstand sin, to reject sin, and to turn from evil whenever it appears in our path.

Those with a wavering commitment to Jesus as Lord repeatedly give in to temptations because they don't have a firm resolve not to sin.

Does this mean that every Christian lives a sin-free life? No. We continue to live in fleshly bodies. We have habits and old routines that we need to change. We have minds that we need to renew by the reading of God's Word. We have hearts that need to be healed by a growing relationship with the Lord. We will sin from time to time in thought, word, and deed, but our desire as genuine Christians must be to follow the Lord closely so that we don't sin, and if we do sin, we immediately recognize that sin, confess it, receive forgiveness for it, and move forward with an even stronger determination not to sin.

Stripping Away All Excuses

What happens when people feel temptation? Why do people give in?

I believe most people who give in to temptation offer one of five excuses.

Excuse #1: Somebody Made Me Do It

The person who gives this excuse is into blaming others instead of taking full responsibility for his own decisions, choices, and behavior.

The first man ever created took this tack. Adam said to God after he had eaten the forbidden fruit of the Tree of the Knowledge of Good and Evil, "The woman whom You gave to be with me, she gave me of the tree, and I ate" (Gen. 3:12). That excuse didn't justify Adam's actions then, and it doesn't justify our yielding to temptation today. Even so, people try again and again to say, "My family talked me into this. My coworkers were doing it. My upbringing didn't give me the strength to resist this temptation. My circumstances set me up to yield to this temptation."

Nobody forces anybody to give in to a temptation. A person may entice you, encourage you, or invite you to sin with him, but that person cannot cause you to engage in sinful behavior. You need to take responsibility for your behavior.

Read what God's Word says about this:

My son, if sinners entice you,
Do not consent.
If they say, "Come with us,
Let us lie in wait to shed blood;
Let us lurk secretly for the innocent
    without cause;
Let us swallow them alive like Sheol,
And whole, like those who go down to
    the Pit;
We shall find all kinds of precious
possessions,
We shall fill our houses with spoil;
Cast in your lot among us,

Let us all have one purse" —
My son, do not walk in the way with
  them,
Keep your foot from their path;
For their feet run to evil,
And they make haste to shed blood.
  (Prov. 1:10–16)

"But," you may be saying, "I would
never be enticed to commit murder so I
can rob a person."

No? But are you subject to others enticing you to drink with them after work
and then drive under the influence of that
alcohol? Are you subject to joining forces
to drive a particular person away from
your company so you can take over his job?
Are you allowing yourself to be enticed to
commit adultery, which may very well result in the death of a marriage and the loss
of material substance for both the innocent
spouse and the guilty one?

The excuses "everybody is doing it" and
"nobody will ever know" just don't fly.
Those who are truly in right standing with
God aren't doing whatever sin you are
being tempted to do, and somebody will
know what you have done — His name is
Jesus Christ.

Excuse #2: God Made Me Do It

The person who offers this excuse believes, in essence, "God could have stopped this temptation from coming my way. Therefore, God sent this temptation."

We need to be very clear on this point: God does not tempt anybody. The Bible tells us,

> Let no one say when he is tempted, "I am tempted by God"; for God cannot be tempted by evil, nor does He Himself tempt anyone. But each one is tempted when he is drawn away by his own desires and enticed. Then, when desire has conceived, it gives birth to sin; and sin, when it is full-grown, brings forth death. Do not be deceived, my beloved brethren. Every good gift and every perfect gift is from above, and comes down from the Father of lights, with whom there is no variation or shadow of turning. Of His own will He brought us forth by the word of truth, that we might be a kind of first fruits of His creatures. (James 1:13–18)

Temptations are not desires to do good or to display righteousness. By its very definition, a temptation is a desire instilled into the heart and mind of a person prompting him to do something that is not good. God will never tempt someone to sin. A person who believes that God causes temptation also must believe that God delights in setting people up for failure — in other words, God plays tricks on people and entices people to do bad things just so He can have fun by punishing them. Nothing could be further from the truth.

The passage from the book of James makes it very clear that we are tempted when we allow ourselves to be drawn away by our own desires.

Some people believe that it's all right to use negative means if they are quick methods to achieving positive goals. In other words, it might be all right to steal from a company that is producing a bad product if it means bringing about the downfall of that company, or if the money is put into programs to help those injured by the company. That isn't God's way. God never leads a person to use an ungodly method for a godly goal. Again, Scripture makes that clear. God has no variation or shadow of turning — every good gift and every perfect gift comes from Him. He brings us forth "by the word of truth," not by trickery, lies, manipulation, or sinful methods.

Excuse #3: God Knows I'm Weak

The person who uses this excuse may not blame God for sending the temptation, but he blames God for his inability to say no to it. The line of reasoning usually goes something like this: "God made me this way. He knows I'm weak in this area. He could have kept this temptation from coming my way."

The truth is, the person who uses this excuse didn't ask for God's help! We all have weaknesses and flaws. The flaws are not excuses for sinning, but reasons for seeking God's help in all things at all times! It is at the point of our weakness that we must become most dependent on God. And the good news of the Bible is this: God will help us resist, or He will make a way out of the temptation for us!

The Bible tells us, "God is faithful, who will not allow you to be tempted beyond what you are able, but with the temptation will also make the way of escape, that you may be able to bear it" (1 Cor. 10:13).

Each of us has the power of choice when it comes to a temptation — we can say no or yes. The more we feel an impulse to give in to temptation, the more we need to turn to the Lord and cry out, "Help me!" He will provide the strength that we lack.

If we will use our free will to ask for God's help, He will supply the power — and that, my friend, is true willpower. It is our will plus His power that gives us an enduring ability to say no to temptation, no matter how strong or frequent the temptation.

God assures us, "Call upon Me in the day of trouble; I will deliver you, and you shall glorify Me" (Ps. 50:15).

Excuse #4: This Is Different

The person who uses this excuse believes that he is being tempted in some unusual way; therefore, the normal rules and commandments of the Bible don't apply to him. He believes he is justified because the temptation "came out of the blue" or "was unlike anything I've ever experienced before."

He may also see the temptation as being sent to him because he is special in some way — either especially marked by God and, therefore, beyond the commandments that apply to all other people, or especially marked by the devil and, therefore, beyond the realm of God's protective power.

Sometimes people will say, "I don't know anybody else who has ever faced this." Or they say, "It didn't seem like a sin at the time. The person told me that what I was doing was permissible and even desirable in God's eyes." Often people will even say, "The person who enticed me with this told me that he was doing God's will or that this was for my good."

The Bible warns, "Let him who thinks he stands take heed lest he fall" (1 Cor. 10:12). In other words, don't ever think that you are beyond the rules of the Bible, or that you have the ability in yourself to determine right and wrong apart from God's Word. Don't ever think that you are beyond being tempted or tricked into doing what is evil.

The Bible also says, "No temptation has overtaken you except such as is common to man" (1 Cor. 10:13). There are no new temptations. What the devil sends to you he has sent to countless other people across the face of the earth, now and through the ages past.

Excuse #5: I've Thought About It, so I Might As Well Do It

One of the devil's lies is that thinking a sinful thought is the same as committing a sinful deed. That simply isn't God's truth. There's a huge difference between thinking a bad thought and committing an act of sin.

"But," you may say, "Jesus taught, for example, that whoever looks at a woman and lusts after her has already committed adultery in his heart." That's right. The person who lusts is entertaining adultery in his heart — he's on a slippery downhill slope. He didn't think just one bad thought; he has allowed that thought to develop into full-blown lust. If he doesn't recognize what he's doing and put a stop to it with God's help, he will eventually take action on his fantasies.

The people to whom Jesus was speaking believed that it didn't matter what a person thought or felt. It only mattered what a person did. Jesus said, "It matters very much what you think and feel because what you think and feel will give rise to what you do. Lust that goes unchecked in a person's heart and mind will produce adulterous behavior. Stop your lusting so you won't commit adultery!"

No person can keep from thinking a negative, wrong, or sinful thought from time to time. Thoughts come. The good thoughts should stick and take root. The negative, wrong, and sinful thoughts need to be released immediately.

Don't entertain any thought that is related to sin. If you entertain a sinful thought long enough, it will erupt in behavior.

Learn How to Resist

Resisting temptation is a learning process. If you are tempted repeatedly in a particular area of your life, I encourage you to go to someone you know who is also tempted in that area and has successfully responded in resisting the temptation and refusing to yield to it. Get the person's best, godly counsel. Learn from his experience.

"But," you may say, "what if I don't know anyone who has successfully resisted temptation?"

We all have the example of Jesus, who was tempted in much stronger ways than any other human being has been or will be tempted.

"Well," you may reply, "Jesus was the Son of God. Of course He could resist temptation."

Let me point out to you a couple of

things you may not have considered about Jesus and the temptations He experienced from Satan in the wilderness. (See Matthew 4:1–11 and Luke 4:1–13.)

First, Jesus was fully human. He had physical and emotional needs as a human being. He did not have the spiritual needs human beings have — He already knew God's love, had no need for forgiveness because He had never sinned, knew with full assurance that He would return to heaven, and He had the abiding presence and power of the Godhead functioning in His life at all times. Even with these needs met, Jesus did have needs for food, water, air, security, and shelter. He did have needs for human fellowship, and He knew that the success of His divine mission meant that He needed to have a certain degree of acceptance and a certain level of fulfillment of His divine purpose to bring about all that He was assigned to do on this earth.

Second, Jesus was perfect in His humanity in ways we aren't. We are born with a sin nature. Jesus was not. That made His temptation by the devil even more grievous to Him than temptations are to us. How so? More was at stake. Remember that a temptation is an enticement to use God-given gifts to gratify God-given desires and drives in an ungodly, wrong way or at a wrong time.

Jesus very much wanted to fulfill His divine desire and drive to win as many people back to the Father as possible, in as short a period of time as possible. His goals were absolute and perfect. No person has ever had such goals or been gifted to achieve those goals.

Jesus had very strong compassion for sinful humanity. He wanted people to be set free from all that held them in bondage — physically, emotionally, mentally, and spiritually. His compassion was greater than that of any other person in history. No person has ever had such absolute and perfect love.

The devil came to Jesus right after God the Father and John the Baptist had affirmed to Him that He was God's beloved Son. The devil began his temptations with the word *if*. He attempted to cast doubt on what Jesus had heard from God the Father and from the most righteous man on earth apart from Jesus. The devil attacked Jesus at the heart of His identity, His strength.

The devil will always strike at who you are in Christ Jesus and what you have been gifted to do, both natural gifts and spiritual gifts. He will say such things as, "Are you really a Christian? If you are really a Christian, you wouldn't do that. If you are really a Christian, you should be able to do this. If you truly have that gift from God, you should be able to . . ."

The devil attempts to call into question your relationship with God and your gifts and identity in Christ Jesus. He attempts to call into question the presence and work of the Holy Spirit in and through your life.

The Devil Presents What Seems Reasonable

The devil first attempted to entice Jesus to do a miracle that would meet His physical need for food in the wilderness. He said, "If You are the Son of God, command that these stones become bread" (Matt. 4:3). That certainly seems like a reasonable thing for Jesus to do. He was alone in the wilderness, fasting for forty days. It seems entirely plausible for Jesus to have turned stones into bread. But to do so would have been to gratify His needs and desires in an inappropriate way. What was inappropriate about it? Jesus would have been responding to a directive and suggestion of the devil. God does not do what the devil entices or tells Him to do!

The Devil Offers Questionable Methods

The devil then appealed to Jesus' need to have a following. The devil tempted Jesus to throw Himself off the pinnacle of the temple to draw attention to Himself by doing a major miracle that would capture everybody's attention and imagination. This temptation presented a questionable methodology. The devil was appealing to Jesus to accomplish His purpose on the earth through certain means that would be quick, flamboyant, and irrefutable. The methodology, however, was not what fulfilled Scripture. It was not God's way for providing atonement for the sins of the whole world. God's methodology required the death of Jesus on the cross.

Another point here is important for you to consider. When the devil issued this temptation to Jesus, he threw in a couple of Bible verses to try to convince Jesus that it really was a good method for Jesus to use. The devil said, "It is written: 'He shall give His angels charge over you,' and, 'In their hands they shall bear you up, lest you dash your foot against a stone' " (Matt. 4:6). The devil was quoting Psalm 91:11–12 to Jesus.

There are times when the devil may remind you of a verse of Scripture or something a godly person has said to you to reinforce his temptation. He will use isolated verses to paint the method he advocates in the most favorable light possible. His purpose is to cause doubt, confusion, and questioning about whether you should employ what you know is God's method or try the devil's method.

For example, a young couple may intend to get married. Along comes the opportunity for them to purchase a home, but the offer is good only a few days. They can't afford the home on just one salary. The devil says, "Move in together. You're going to get married anyway. What difference does it make if you live together now? Just look around. Lots of couples are living together before they get married. By living together, you can afford the house you want."

The goals are godly. There's certainly nothing ungodly about marriage. There's nothing ungodly about owning a home. But the method is all wrong in light of God's Word!

The Devil Never Presents the Right Timetable

The devil appealed to Jesus on the

matter of timing. Jesus knew that the kingdoms of the earth were His ultimately. He knew that what He did on the cross would seal His authority over the kingdoms of the earth. What the devil tempted Jesus to do was to secure those kingdoms without any ministry or suffering. The devil said, "All these things I will give You right now if You will fall down and worship me." That was entirely wrong on two accounts. First, the devil did not have the authority to give all the kingdoms to Jesus, not eternally. Second, the devil was attempting to keep Jesus from doing the one thing that would secure the kingdoms of the earth for Jesus — which was the sacrifice of His blood and death on the cross. He was trying to trip up Jesus on timing.

The devil will come to you with temptations that seem reasonable. His temptations always sound like a good idea when taken at a surface level.

The devil will come to you with clever, creative ideas that, upon closer examination, will be shown to be questionable. He comes with suggestions for methods and means that seem to be effective — maybe so, maybe not. Perhaps, but perhaps not.

The devil will come to you with temptations that are totally wrong when it comes to timing. He will tell you that he can give you something that he truly cannot give you. The devil's timing is never the right timing. The devil's claim to being able to do something eternally good is never a valid claim!

How Jesus Responded to Temptation

Jesus is our role model. The way He responded to temptation is the way we are to respond to it.

So how did Jesus respond to the devil's temptations?

He dealt with each temptation in exactly the same way. He quoted the Word of God to the devil. If this method was good enough to be used by Jesus, it's a method good enough for any of us to use!

When the devil said, "If You are the Son of God, command that these stones become bread," Jesus answered by quoting Deuteronomy 8:3, "It is written, 'Man shall not live by bread alone, but by every word that proceeds from the mouth of God.'" (See Matthew 4:3–4.) Jesus said, in quoting this verse from the Old Testament, "God has a way to meet My physical needs as a human being. I am a man, and I trust God the Father to meet My human needs."

When the devil said, "Throw Yourself down" from the pinnacle of the temple, Jesus replied by quoting Deuteronomy 6:16, "It is written again, 'You shall not tempt the LORD your God.'" (See Matthew 4:6–7.) Jesus replied to the devil's misuse of Scripture with an irrefutable absolute that was part of God's law. He was striking a blow at the devil's claim to have a valid methodology. The truth is, God's methods work for God's goals. The devil's methods never produce anything that is eternally beneficial. Jesus was speaking very specifically to the devil in this moment, "You shall not tempt the Lord your God." The devil had no God-given authority whatsoever to tempt Jesus to use this method.

When the devil offered Jesus all the kingdoms of the world and their glory, Jesus replied, "Away with you, Satan! For it is written, 'You shall worship the LORD your God, and Him only you shall serve'" (Matt. 4:10). Jesus was again quoting from the Old Testament — this time Deuteronomy 6:13. He sent the devil away by reminding the devil that he was under orders from God the Father to worship only God and to serve only Him. The devil was the one who needed to be worshiping Jesus and serving Him!

The Pattern of Our Response

What does this mean to us? The temptation of Jesus in the wilderness gives us the pattern of response we are to use when the devil tempts us.

First and foremost, there's no substitute for replying to the devil's temptations with a verbal, spoken-aloud quote of the Word of God. Eve entered into a conversation with the devil and yielded to temptation. Jesus replied with a command from Scripture and did not yield to temptation. It's as simple as that. Don't discuss anything with the devil. Quote God's Word to him.

There is no substitute for knowing the Word of God. The less you know, the more susceptible you are to the devil's temptations. It is vitally important that you read, study, and memorize the Word of God so you have verses of Scripture already planted in your heart and mind when temptations arise. If you have done this, the Holy Spirit can bring those verses to your remembrance quickly. They become a powerful reply to temptation. Your voicing of those verses with a commanding tone of voice will send the devil fleeing and, at the same time, allow the Holy Spirit of God to minister to you and strengthen you.

Second, Jesus stood on the promises of God that God would meet all of His needs as a human being. You need to know those promises and stand on them as well.

Third, Jesus was 100 percent committed and resolved in His heart and mind that He would choose to do things God's way — using God's methods to achieve God's goals — and to act in God's timing. Throughout His ministry, Jesus said repeatedly that He did only what He saw the Father doing, when He saw the Father doing it.

This is something you need to settle in your heart and mind. You must come to the place where you are 100 percent committed to doing things God's way and in God's timing.

Distancing Yourself from the Tempter

In dealing with the devil, Jesus commanded him, "Away with you" (Matt. 4:10). Jesus, in effect, distanced Himself from the tempter.

Sometimes you may not have either the time or the opportunity to respond to your tempter with the Word of God. This is especially true if a temptation comes to you through a human being. Suddenly you may be in a situation that you know is evil or is headed for sin. In those times it is no less important that you distance yourself from the devil — in those cases, however, you need to be the one who walks away.

Consider what happened in the life of Joseph when Potiphar's wife "cast longing eyes on Joseph" and said to him, "Lie with me." (See Genesis 39:7.)

The devil knew this man's God-given gifts and desires. He knew that God had given Joseph two dreams that foretold his future greatness. The devil didn't have any secret knowledge about those dreams. All he had to do was overhear Joseph telling his brothers about those dreams. The devil could also see what everybody else could see: "Joseph was handsome in form and appearance" (Gen. 39:6).

The devil also knew the hatred, jealousy, and rejection Joseph had experienced by his brothers — all of which had culminated in Joseph's being sold into slavery in Egypt. He knew the deep needs that Joseph no doubt had for love, acceptance, and recognition.

The devil knew Joseph's success in the house of Potiphar. Joseph had risen to the position of overseer of Potiphar's estate. Everything Joseph had touched turned to success. Everything he had attempted prospered. Joseph had found such favor in Potiphar's sight that everything in Potiphar's household was put under his authority.

I have no doubt that the devil reminded Joseph of his physical neediness. He was a young man without a wife, with normal physical and sexual needs and desires.

I have no doubt that the devil played upon the needs of Joseph for appreciation, love, and acceptance. Joseph was a young slave in the foreign land of Egypt, far from his family and his people.

I have no doubt that the devil set up the situation so that Joseph was alone in the house with Potiphar's wife. I have no doubt that the devil said to Joseph, "You have everything else under your authority in Potiphar's house. You should have everything in your control, including Potiphar's wife. She's available. She's willing. You have needs. Seize this moment. Nobody will ever know."

The devil was attempting to get Joseph

to use his God-given abilities to meet his God-given desires and needs in an ungodly way right then.

When Potiphar's wife caught Joseph by his garment, physically touching him as she once again said, "Lie with me," Joseph did not argue with her or try to talk to her. He "fled and ran outside" (Gen. 39:12).

There may be times when a temptation comes to you through another person and there's no time to quote Scripture to that person. You must respond in that moment by fleeing. Walk away. Get out of the person's presence as fast as you can. Don't worry about being rude or politically incorrect. Get out of the tempter's presence.

If you can't send the tempter away by resisting him and quoting God's Word to him, then get away from the tempter physically as quickly as you can!

The Best Time to Say No to a Temptation

The best time to say no to a temptation is immediately!

Don't wait for the temptation to come again. Don't give in to a temptation with the attitude, "I'll try this once, but only once. Next time I'll say no."

God warns us about the dangers and consequences of yielding to temptation. He warns us in His Word. He warns us through godly people. He warns us through the examples of people or through experiences in our lives.

Don't ignore God's warnings!

Samson did.

Samson had a weakness for Philistine women. I don't know exactly what about them was attractive to Samson — the Bible doesn't tell us. He went to a Philistine town, Timnah, and saw a Philistine woman there. He came home saying to his father and mother, "I have seen a woman in Timnah of the daughters of the Philistines; now therefore, get her for me as a wife." (See Judges 14:1–2.)

Samson's parents knew that God had a call on Samson's life. Samson had been destined from before his birth to be a Nazarite — a man set apart for God's plans and purposes. As good Israelites, Samson's parents also knew that he should marry an Israelite girl. They replied to Samson's request, "Is there no woman among the daughters of your brethren, or among all my people, that you must go and get a wife from the uncircumcised

Philistines?" (Judg. 14:3).

Samson was an adult, however. He could make his own choice, and he refused to heed the Word of God or the advice of his parents. He insisted, "Get her for me, for she pleases me well" (Judg. 14:3).

When this desire of Samson's resulted in his chosen bride being given to someone else, the death of thirty men of Ashkelon, and ultimately his chosen bride's death, Samson returned home to his parents.

Did Samson learn from this experience with the young woman in Timnah? No.

Samson next turned to a harlot in Gaza, also a Philistine area. The Philistines got word that he was with the harlot, and Samson narrowly missed being killed.

Did Samson learn from this experience with the harlot in Gaza? No.

Samson next turned to a Philistine woman named Delilah. She repeatedly tricked Samson, and he continued to stick around through three temptations aimed at stripping him of his physical power. He allowed himself to be bound with seven fresh bowstrings, then he allowed himself to be bound with new ropes, and then he allowed Delilah to weave his hair into the web of a loom. Each time Samson was able to free himself and defeat those who came to destroy him. Each time Samson stayed around to entertain Delilah's next temptation.

Finally Samson gave in to Delilah's insistent pleas to tell her the source of his strength. He allowed her to cut his hair, and that time he was captured. His eyes were gouged from his head, and he was bound with bronze fetters and made to turn the wheel of a huge stone that ground grain. He was forced to walk in circles day after day, month after month, totally enslaved by his archenemies.

Samson's life is a picture of what happens when we willfully choose to ignore God's warnings.

Don't dismiss what God commands in His Word. His commandments are intended to safeguard you from evil.

Don't dismiss what godly parents counsel you to do. Their wise counsel is for your protection.

Don't dismiss or discount the ways in which God has spared you from evil in the past. Recognize His loving hand at work in your life, sparing you from evil and its consequences.

Don't think you are above the attempts of the enemy to trip you up or entice you. Don't think that you can outmaneuver the devil or outsmart those in whom the devil operates. He is crafty, wily, manipulative, and subtle beyond human measure.

Don't play with fire.

Those who do eventually get burned.

If you fail to heed God's repeated warnings, you are likely to find yourself enslaved by the very forces that you thought you could control or conquer. You are likely to find yourself on an addictive treadmill, living a life that is without godly purpose, joy, or deep emotional satisfaction.

God's warnings are there. He never fails to warn His people about the consequences associated with evil. He always holds out the wonderful promises associated with obedience. Listen to what God speaks to you in the Bible, through godly people, and through your own prior experiences.

9

Staying Dressed for Battle

A friend told me about a practice that she and her brother adopted when they were fairly young children. Their family went to the beach each summer for the Fourth of July weekend. She and her brother looked forward to this minivacation every year — it was a highlight of the summer. At the beach, the family had picnics and a cookout on the sand. They had the same cabin every summer, and their cousins had the adjacent cabin. They had shell-gathering contests, and over the course of several summers, they had learned to swim in the surf and identify dozens of creatures in the tidal pools.

"We loved this weekend at the beach so much that my brother and I always went to bed the night before with our beach clothes on underneath our pajamas," she said. "We wanted to be fully ready when Mom and Dad called us in the morning. We were out the door within seconds after they awoke us. I don't think they ever really knew what we had done — they always seemed amazed that we were dressed so quickly."

Dressed and ready to go. That's what the Bible tells us to be — in a spiritual dimension — when it comes to facing our enemy!

One of the most important passages in the Bible about overcoming enemy attacks is found in Ephesians 6:10–18. I encourage you to read this passage carefully and then to mark this place in your book so you can refer to it readily.

> Finally, my brethren, be strong in the Lord and in the power of His might. Put on the whole armor of God, that you may be able to stand against the wiles of the devil. For we do not wrestle against flesh and blood, but against principalities, against powers, against the rulers of the darkness of this age, against spiritual hosts of wickedness in the heavenly places.
>
> Therefore take up the whole armor of God, that you may be able to withstand in the evil day, and having done all, to stand.
>
> Stand therefore, having girded your waist with truth, having put on the breastplate of righteousness, and having

shod your feet with the preparation of the gospel of peace; above all, taking the shield of faith with which you will be able to quench all the fiery darts of the wicked one. And take the helmet of salvation, and the sword of the Spirit, which is the word of God; praying always with all prayer and supplication in the Spirit, being watchful to this end with all perseverance and supplication for all the saints.

We need to be ready for potential battle at all times. Why? Because we simply don't know when or where the devil is going to strike at us. Don't be lulled into thinking that because everything is fine today, everything will automatically be fine tomorrow. The devil never gives up trying to defeat you. He's always looking for your blind side and your weak moment. It is foolishness to wait until the enemy strikes to prepare for a potential battle. The truth is, it's often too late to get adequately prepared for battle after a battle has begun!

In writing to the Ephesians, Paul mentioned the "evil day." To what was he referring?

The "evil day" described the most intense moments of Satan's attacks and temptations. It was a reference not to a particular time on the calendar of history, but to the intensity with which the devil attacks every person from time to time. These are the moments and days that we tend to call crises or tragedies. Sometimes these crises come to us after a slow buildup over time. The river is rising, and suddenly the dikes no longer hold back the water. The storm is coming, and suddenly it hits with fury. The relationship is degenerating, and suddenly there's a subpoena to appear in family court. The anger is building, and suddenly it erupts.

Sometimes these moments strike us as sudden emergencies. The house catches on fire; the child is abducted; the building is attacked; the person is taken hostage.

Whether the moment is slow or fast in coming, the moment requires vitally important decision making on our part. The evil day brings with it the absolute necessity of making the right choice or decision because the entire future, and sometimes the eternal future, rests on the actions we take.

Every person has evil days. Nobody is immune from them.

How are we to resist? By putting on the "whole armor of God."

We put on this armor daily so that we are ready for the devil's attacks. Every soldier knows that the time to put on armor is before the attack, not after an attack begins. The devil always seeks to attack us from our blind side, the least anticipated aspect of our lives. We don't see him coming; therefore, we need to be ready for whatever he throws at us, whenever that moment occurs.

The battle pieces of armor that Paul described are like the pieces of armor worn by a Roman soldier, but if we step back and see this armor in a spiritual light, we quickly recognize that the armor is the nature and likeness of Christ Jesus. We are to put on or clothe ourselves in the righteousness and power that are rightfully the Lord's. We have the ability to put on these attributes of Christ Jesus because we have put our trust in Him as our Savior and Lord. He dwells in us by the power of His Holy Spirit, and we are given the power to become "more than conquerors." (See Romans 8:37.)

The Belt of Truth

The apostle Paul wrote that you are to

stand "having girded your waist with truth" (Eph. 6:14).

Roman soldiers wore a long tunic that was cinched in at the waist by a belt so they could move quickly and decisively without tripping over the garment. The belt was wide; it extended down from the waist to cover the abdomen and, in some designs, the groin area. The belt had a place to attach a sword.

We are wise to ask about this passage in Ephesians: Why did Paul assign certain aspects of Christ Jesus to specific parts of the physical body?

I don't believe it's an accident, for example, that Paul assigned truth to the lower abdominal area, or righteousness to the upper-body area. Various parts of the body are vulnerable in different ways to physical injury. The same is true for the whole of our lives — each of us is subject to various types of error and attack, at different times, in different ways, with different results.

The abdomen was considered the most vulnerable area in a sword fight because it was soft and fleshy tissue. A sword could penetrate the abdomen easily, and wounds to this area were prone to intense and often uncontrollable bleeding. Abdominal wounds were highly susceptible to infection. Abdominal wounds very often led to death — immediate death in battle as a result of bleeding, or death soon after the battle as a result of infection.

What is the first piece of armor we have in strongly resisting temptation or evil? The girdle of truth!

What are the organs of the physical body located in the abdominal area? First, the organs related to the digestion of food and elimination of waste are located in this area. Second, the organs of reproduction are in this area.

Paul was saying to the Ephesians, "You have to know what to take into your life and what to eliminate from your life. Truth must be the filter for all perceptions, ideas, and dreams."

Can you see how vital this is? If you are entertaining ideas based upon false information or lies, you are living in a state of delusion. If you are basing your dreams on a lie, you are not only deluded, but you are also likely living in illusion. You are believing what isn't real and what cannot be. If you are unsure about what is true and what is a lie, you will be living in a state of confusion, and your decisions and choices will lack clarity, focus, and power.

God does not desire for His people to live in delusion, illusion, or confusion! He wants us to be quick to sift through the thousands of images and ideas and sensory perceptions that bombard us every day and say with definitive authority and clarity, "This lines up with God's truth. This does not line up."

The things that are true, we are to take into our lives and make a part of us — we are to think on them, believe them, adopt them as our attitudes, and live by them as our guiding principles. The things that are not true, we are to eliminate quickly. They are a waste of time, energy, and attention.

But what is the relationship to our organs of reproduction? These organs are linked to our relationships. Everything that is birthed on this earth — not only physical babies, but ideas, ministries, companies, movements, and organizations — is birthed in relationship with other people. We need to know which relationships are based on God's truth and which are rooted in lies. We need to develop relationships that are based on God's truth and that function in honesty, integrity, purity, vulnerability, mutual sharing and support, and genuine love and respect. Relationships that are based on a lie function according to manipulation, deceit, pride, grasping greediness, and the concept "Do unto others before they have a chance to do unto you."

I cannot overemphasize how important it is that you form alliances — including whom you date or choose as a marriage partner — based upon truth. So many times through the years a young husband or wife has said to me, "I didn't know . . ."

Sometimes the spouse didn't know about the other person's past, a drinking or drug habit, or the spiritual commitment to Christ (or lack of one). Sometimes the spouse didn't know how wrapped up the person was in an old relationship or how manipulated the person was by a parent who couldn't let go. When the truth came to light, the unsuspecting spouse was devastated. It was as if he had married a person he didn't really know. The lines I have heard so often are, "I don't really know him anymore," or "She just isn't who I thought she was."

People tell lies. And sometimes people just live a lie. Not all lies are spoken. We may need to evaluate what isn't being said or what isn't being done. We need to see clearly the character of a person, because truth telling and living in truth are vital to the success of any friendship, business partnership, marriage, or any other relationship that is linked to long-term godly goals.

The pursuit of truth requires a real commitment on our part. We must be intentional about pursuing truth.

Again, it's no accident that truth is linked to the things we take into our lives or the relationships we forge. Eating is intentional. So is a sexual relationship or any relationship designed to birth something in the natural, financial, or spiritual realm. We must be intentional about what we choose to see and hear and take into our lives. We must be intentional about the people we choose to hang out with, be around, associate with, go places with, and so forth. We must make a continual choice to take only God's best into our lives and associate only with those who are following the Lord with their whole hearts, minds, and souls.

Does this mean we should never associate with an unbeliever? No. But our purpose for associating with an unbeliever should be to share Christ with that person. Our purpose should not be to date that person, marry that person, go into business with that person, live with that person, invest with that person, and so forth. God's

Word is very clear on this:

> Do not be unequally yoked together with unbelievers. For what fellowship has righteousness with lawlessness? And what communion has light with darkness? And what accord has Christ with Belial? Or what part has a believer with an unbeliever? And what agreement has the temple of God with idols? For you are the temple of the living God. As God has said:
>
> "I will dwell in them
> And walk among them.
> I will be their God,
> And they shall be My people."
> Therefore
> "Come out from among them
> And be separate, says the Lord.
> Do not touch what is unclean,
> And I will receive you.
> I will be a Father to you,
> And you shall be My sons and
>   daughters,
> Says the LORD Almighty."
>   (2 Cor. 6:14–18)

(See also Isaiah 52:11; Ezekiel 20:34, 41; 2 Samuel 7:14.)

At the very heart of your being intentional about living in the truth — about putting this girdle of truth around you — is your conscious commitment to trust Jesus as your Savior and make a commitment to believe in Him and follow Him with your whole heart. A commitment is a very serious matter. It's saying, "I will follow Jesus as the Lord of my life no matter what."

Do you know the truth of God's unconditional love?

Do you know the truth that you are eternally secure?

Do you know the truth that you are saved by His grace, not by your works?

You must stand for the truth without compromise.

Furthermore, a person cannot live the Christian life with consistency and victory if he does not make a commitment to pursue the truth of God's Word. You must know the commandments and principles of God. The commandments and principles are there in the Bible for you to read, but you must make the intentional effort to read the Bible and to reread it day in and day out, year in and year out, so those commandments and principles become a part of you. You must fully take them into your spirit so that your responses, choices, and decisions are almost automatic according to God's Word.

When you are faced with a decision, an evaluation, a choice, an option, your first thoughts become, *Is this in line with God's Word? Am I being presented with the whole truth? Does this in any way violate or contradict my relationship with Jesus as my Savior? Does this conform to the truth of God's love?* It is in this way that truth, based on God's Word, becomes the filter for every decision, every relationship, and every choice. Eventually these thoughts aren't even conscious — they are instinctual.

Truth ultimately is a person — Jesus Christ. In putting on truth, we are putting on Christ. Each of us says, "I am in Christ. Christ is in me, and because Christ is in me by the power of His Holy Spirit, Christ's truth is in me." Putting on the girdle of truth is proclaiming that we have the truth of God — it is available to us, it is part of us, and it is operating in us at all times.

The Breastplate of Righteousness

The apostle Paul wrote that you are to stand "having put on the breastplate of righteousness" (Eph. 6:14).

In the times of Roman rule, the breastplates of soldiers were usually made of thick leather. They didn't provide the full metal protection of breastplates in the Middle Ages or later, but the breastplates did keep many arrows and swords and knives from full penetration into a soldier's flesh.

And what did a breastplate cover? The vital organs of a soldier — especially the heart and lungs. It was extremely important since a puncture to the heart and lungs meant instant death.

What does it mean to be "righteous"?

The Bible tells us that when we accept Jesus as our Savior, we receive the "gift" of righteousness (Rom. 5:17; 2 Cor. 5:21). This gift of righteousness is imputed righteousness. The righteousness we receive is Christ's righteousness, not our own righteousness. We stand in a position, "I am in Christ. Christ is in me. And because Christ is in me by the power of His Holy Spirit, I have Christ's righteousness available to me and operating within me."

The righteousness that Paul described in this passage to the Ephesians is a practical, daily righteousness — it is walking and living according to what is right before God. The word for righteousness in this passage refers to a lining up of a person's beliefs, attitudes, thoughts, and behavior with God's commandments and principles.

There simply is no substitute for living obediently before God.

Just as we are the ones who determine what we will allow into our lives, so, too, we are the ones who determine whether we will seek daily to be cleansed of sin and to pursue the will of God. The heart's desire must be to live in a way that is pleasing and honoring to God. It is to have a heart once "bent" toward sin that is now "bent" toward the things of God. It is to say as King David said, "Create in me a clean heart, O God. And renew a steadfast spirit within me" (Ps. 51:10).

For years, I've heard the phrase "living a nominally Christian life." Friend, there is no such thing! A person who is walking in the flesh tolerates sin and excuses, rationalizes, and justifies sin. The person may be saved, but he isn't walking in obedience to Jesus as Lord. Therefore, he is not living a Christian life. He is not living a life that is representative of Christ or that reflects Christ to a sinful world. To live a genuinely Christian life, a person must make an intentional decision for righteousness — he must "put on" the righteousness of Christ and choose to walk every day in a way that is pleasing to the Lord. He must choose to obey God's commandments.

This decision for righteousness must become as automatic in our lives as breathing in and breathing out.

Let's focus on what it might mean for the breastplate of righteousness to cover a person's lungs and heart — in the natural and in the spiritual.

The lungs connect us to our environment in a unique way. We breathe in the world around us. We exhale into the world around us. The world contributes to us, and we contribute to the world. If the air we breathe is poisonous or polluted, our bodies eventually suffer. In like manner, if we continually put ourselves in evil, unwholesome, negative environments, we cannot help breathing in that spiritual environment. We can pollute our spirits.

As a pastor, I am very concerned, of course, with people who breathe in false teachings about Jesus and about God's Word. If a person puts himself into the spiritual environment of a church or other group that preaches, "You don't need Jesus as your Savior — any spiritual path will do"; "God doesn't exist, just love"; "You can have anything you want in this life if you'll just say that you have it"; "You can live any way you want on Saturday night and then ask God's forgiveness on Sunday morning and it will all be okay," that person is choosing to breathe into his spirit what amounts to spiritual poison.

People routinely listen to all kinds of music with messages that amount to spiritual pollution. They go to clubs and parties that are cesspools when it comes to the things of God. They listen to filthy jokes and stories, watch unwholesome movies and television programs, and surf through sinful Web sites on the Internet, taking into their minds and hearts pure unrighteousness. All of these things go straight into the heart and mind, where they act as poison.

You can't put yourself into an environment or atmosphere of continual unrighteousness and expect the breastplate of Christ's righteousness to negate what you willfully choose to breathe into your spirit!

And what do you exhale into the world? What are you saying to your immediate environment — the environment of your home, your workplace, your church? What do people anticipate will come out of you when you are in the committee meeting, in a small group, or at the dinner table?

Do you exhale vehement hate or profound love?

Do you exhale cynicism and sarcasm or appreciation and praise?

Do you exhale an attitude of bitterness or of gratefulness?

Do you exhale anger and pain or the healing balm of kindness?

Do you exhale revenge or mercy?

Do you exhale a seething silence or a vulnerable willingness to reach out to others?

The way you hold your body, your facial gestures, your physical expressions, and the inflection of your voice are part of what you exhale to the world — very often just as much a part of what you give to the world as the words you say and the deeds you do.

Do you give reluctantly and stingily or quickly and generously?

Do you respond with an air of pride or with humility?

Do you fear and distrust others, or are you open and eager to receive their good ideas?

What you exhale into the world must be covered by righteousness, no less so than what you inhale from the world.

The Old Testament has many references to the "breath" of God — from the opening lines of Genesis onward. God's breath into us is always pure. It creates something in us that God calls "good." It produces life and energy. We cannot live a successful Christian life without daily taking into our lives the breath of God's Holy Spirit. We must have the Holy Spirit functioning in us to live a holy life — we simply cannot live in righteousness by our own strength.

Put yourself in an environment where the Holy Spirit can speak to you — as you read God's Word without distraction, as you hear the accurately preached Word of God, as you hear God's Word in uplifting Christian music and messages, or as you listen to tapes of God's Word in your car.

And what about the heart, the other vital organ covered by the breastplate of righteousness? The "heart" refers to the seat of a person's will, and also to the emotions, beliefs, and attitudes that feed into what a person wills or chooses.

Righteousness is to cover all of our emotions, beliefs, and attitudes.

We are to have the "right" feelings and

emotional responses.

We are to have the "right" beliefs.

We are to have the "right" attitudes.

We are to feel, respond emotionally, believe, and have the attitudes that Jesus had. As Paul wrote to the Philippians, "Let this mind be in you which was also in Christ Jesus" (Phil. 2:5). We are to feel, respond emotionally, believe, and have the attitudes that are described in God's Word.

Hate or love?

Anger or gentleness?

Bitterness and resentment or forgiveness?

Which are the "right" feelings and emotional responses we are to have?

God loves me, desires to forgive me, and wants to live with me forever, or God hates me, can never forgive what I've done, and is just waiting to judge me and send me to hell. Which is the "right" set of beliefs?

Racial prejudice or acceptance of others regardless of race?

Hatred for people of other nations or love for people in other nations?

A desire to help and nurture or a desire to tear down and inflict harm?

Which are the "right" attitudes?

The heart pumps the blood that gives life to every cell of the body. And in like manner, what you feel, believe, and hold as an attitude gives life to your words and your actions. The connection is just as automatic as the heart pumping blood beat after beat. If your attitudes, emotions, and beliefs are right, then your words and behavior are going to be right. If your attitudes, emotions, and beliefs are sinful, your words and behavior will be sinful.

God's Word states plainly:

Keep your heart with all diligence,
For out of it spring the issues of life.
Put away from you a deceitful mouth,
And put perverse lips far from you.
Let your eyes look straight ahead,
And your eyelids look right before you.
(Prov. 4:23–25)

God's call to us is to live in righteousness! His righteousness is to cover all that we breathe into our spirits, breathe out to the world, and all of the attitudes, beliefs, and feelings that give rise to our behavior.

Protecting What Is Vital

I mentioned earlier that the breastplate covers the vital organs of the heart and lungs. A person cannot live if the heart is penetrated by a sword or arrow, or if the lungs are punctured by an enemy weapon. Death is immediate, and efforts of resuscitation are rarely successful.

How does this relate to the spiritual life?

What you take in from the world, what you breathe out into the world, and what you say and do based on what you believe, think, and feel — all contribute to something we call integrity.

A person's reputation — integrity, character appraisal in the eyes of others — is directly related to the atmosphere in which he chooses to live and he helps to create, and to what he believes, thinks, feels, says, and does.

Consider any great leader in either the secular world or the church. If you discover that this person steeps himself in a sinful environment, contributes to a sinful environment, or holds sinful attitudes, beliefs, and feelings, what happens to your evaluation of that person? You lose respect for him, don't you? Something about his integrity is damaged. His reputation is tainted.

It doesn't take much to mortally "wound" a person's integrity or reputation. In fact, the higher the person's profile in any group or society, the more vulnerable he is to the damage that can occur as the result of just one indiscretion or one blatantly sinful act or lie.

Some people in leadership positions seem to believe that because they were chosen by God for leadership, certain rules in God's Word no longer apply to them — they see themselves as being above the commandments or believe that, because they have the special responsibilities and pressures of leadership, God does not expect them to strictly keep all of His commandments. That is never the case! God requires leaders, especially, to adhere to His commandments.

At all times, our integrity and reputations are at stake. In other words, our witness for Christ is on the line. The world expects those who claim Christ as their Savior to live morally pure, righteous lives. And when those who claim to be Christians live impure, unholy, degrading lives — or when they are associated with hurtful, sinful attitudes, beliefs, and deeds — the world has little regard for anything they say about Jesus being the Savior.

Now, no person can live a life 100 percent free of mistakes, errors, or sins. We are human beings. But we can be quick to repent of our sins, seek forgiveness, make amends, and adjust our lives so that we don't sin. We can set ourselves to live righteous lives and to seek to be covered daily in all areas that are vital to our integrity and reputations. We can walk in righteousness. We read in 1 John:

My little children, these things I write to you, so that you may not sin. And if anyone sins, we have an Advocate with the Father, Jesus Christ the righteous. And He Himself is the propitiation for our sins, and not for ours only but also for the whole world. (2:1–2)

Little children, abide in Him, that when He appears, we may have confidence and not be ashamed before Him at His coming. If you know that He is righteous, you know that everyone who practices righteousness is born of Him. (2:28–29)

We know that whoever is born of God does not sin; but he who has been born of God keeps himself. (5:18)

Shoes of Preparation of the Gospel of Peace

The apostle Paul wrote that you are to

stand "having shod your feet with the preparation of the gospel of peace" (Eph. 6:15).

No Roman soldier would go into battle without shoes, which were actually thick-soled boots. Shoes enabled a soldier to walk over all sorts of terrain and also to make long marches — moving farther and faster to surprise an enemy. The boots had metal in them that allowed a soldier to hold his footing on slippery slopes or uneven surfaces. Through the years, several experts on war have noted that the Romans were able to conquer so much territory partially because the Roman soldiers had adequate shoes!

The "gospel of peace" does not mean getting ready to preach. Neither does the "gospel of peace" refer to peace between two people or peace between two nations. It refers to the good news of Jesus' provision for our peace with God.

The message of Paul is this: we are to stand firm, grounded in the fact that we have the peace of God in our hearts. We know who we are in Christ Jesus. We don't have to prove ourselves to anybody — we know we are assured of Christ's forgiveness, we know we are loved by God, and we know that we have a secure home in heaven forever.

One of the worst things we can do is to go into a battle against the devil with fear in our hearts. Fear disables and paralyzes. Fear keeps us from taking the decisive action that wins a spiritual battle. Fear clouds the memory and keeps us from making sound, rational, Bible-based decisions. Rather, we are to face the devil with the calm assurance that Jesus knows all about the situation and has already defeated the devil.

Part of the preparation of the gospel of peace is a preparation to face death, which is inevitable for every person. We need to be prepared to face persecution, which is something that all Christians should expect. We need to be prepared to face hard times, which happen to all people. But the gospel — the good news in all this — is that we face these times of trial and difficulty with a deep, inner peace that comes only from knowing that we are grounded in our relationship with Christ Jesus and nothing can destroy that relationship.

Certainly at times the battlefields of our lives are littered with arrow tips and sharp pieces of shrapnel and war debris — such things as an unexpected bill, a lawsuit, an accident, a sudden illness, a breakdown of a piece of equipment, and so forth. Our paths are strewn with rocks and even boulders of problems big and small. We must have peace to walk through a day, from the time we get up in the morning to the time we go to bed at night — we must have a calm steadiness about us if we are to go wherever Christ leads us and do whatever Christ asks of us.

I want to point out three special things to you about this statement, "having shod your feet with the preparation of the gospel of peace."

First, you are the one who accepts into your life the fact that Jesus is your peace. Yet again, your stance is, "I am in Christ. Christ is in me. Christ is the Prince of Peace, and His peace, therefore, is resident and available to me." You must actively accept His peace — recognize it, appropriate it, and apply it to your life.

In other words, when you are faced with angry words, you respond with kind words. When insults are hurled your way, you respond with gentleness. When you face sharp criticism, you listen quietly and respond with mercy and forgiveness. You don't fly off the handle or get uptight when you are tripped up or when someone comes your way to do you harm.

You walk in peace. The apostle Paul

wrote this: "Be anxious for nothing, but in everything by prayer and supplication, with thanksgiving, let your requests be made known to God; and the peace of God, which surpasses all understanding, will guard your hearts and minds through Christ Jesus" (Phil. 4:6).

Second, you are the one who must set your mind and heart in advance of adversity to respond with peace. There's an old saying that some people have a chip on their shoulder. They always seem to be looking for a fight. Some people seem to delight in stirring up trouble, sparking a controversy, engaging in an argument. They simply like to live in conflict. It gives them a sense of power and control — a sense of keeping other people off guard.

To be shod with the preparation of the gospel of peace is to do the exact opposite. It is to develop and exhibit a desire to take God's peace into every situation a person might encounter. A person who has prepared himself to extend the good news of peace walks into every room, every meeting, every home, every appointment, every conference room, and every auditorium with the intent and desire that he will bring God's peace into that place.

God's Word says:

> Ponder the path of your feet,
> And let all your ways be established.
> Do not turn to the right or the left;
> Remove your foot from evil.
>   (Prov. 4:26–27)

In various places in the New Testament, the apostle Paul referred to the "race" he had been called by God to run, or to the "walk" of the believer. Always, we are to run our race and walk out our relationships with God with peace. The fact is, if a person doesn't have peace, he won't leave the house or set out to run any race! Without peace in his heart, he won't take the risk of sharing the gospel with someone or speaking up in a group that is ridiculing the things of God. Without peace reigning in his life, he won't set out for a mission field, give sacrificially, or take an unpopular stand for Christ.

Peace is the bedrock foundation for courage, confidence, and risk-taking in your witness of Jesus Christ to this world. Without peace, you have to work up courage — you have to motivate yourself to have confidence. But with peace filling your heart and motivating your steps, you automatically have confidence and courage.

Third and finally, your goal as someone who has been shod with the preparation of the gospel of peace is to see other people experience the peace of God in their hearts. The goal is to see other people — sinners as well as believers who are experiencing fear, anxiety, or worry — come to such an assurance of Christ's presence and power that the peace of God wells up in them.

Just as is true for righteousness and truth, peace is a person — Jesus is our Peace. In preparing yourself to walk through your days on this earth, you choose to walk where Jesus leads you to walk and to walk as Jesus would walk.

Always On!

The three pieces of the whole armor of God that we have discussed thus far are essentials. They are to be constants in our lives.

A Roman soldier never took off his belt, his breastplate, or his shoes. Even during rest periods or lulls in a battle, a soldier kept on these three essentials.

In like manner, truth, righteousness, and peace are the three essentials of the Christian's armor against the devil. If you know the truth and base all of your relationships and beliefs on the truth, if you are committed to making choices and decisions that keep you in right standing with God at all times, and if you are so grounded in peace that you can walk with assurance and confidence into any situation, you are well armed!

The apostle Paul wrote,

- "having girded your waist"
- "having put on the breastplate"
- "having shod your feet"

The tense of these phrases conveys the message that these elements of your relationship with Christ Jesus are to be at the forefront of your readiness to do battle against the enemy. Let me phrase these three pieces of armor as questions:

Are you filtering every perception and every idea through the filter of truth as evident in Christ Jesus and in the Bible?

Are you asking about each decision and choice you make, "Is this right in God's eyes?"

Are you setting yourself to walk in peace,

always asking, "What can I do to help this person experience more of Jesus' peace in his life?"

The person who lives with this perspective and spiritual attitude is "strong in the Lord and in the power of His might."

But there's more. Paul admonished the Ephesians to "take up" three things.

10

"Taking Up" Armor

There is something very intentional and meaningful about "taking up" arms. To take up a weapon is not a careless or random act. A seriousness and a sense of immediacy are associated with picking up or strapping on a weapon.

The same is true of the spiritual armor that the apostle Paul described to the Ephesians: "taking the shield of faith" and taking "the helmet of salvation, and the sword of the Spirit" (Eph. 6:16–17).

There's a sense that the battle is imminent; the urgency is great. These weapons of our warfare are especially important, I believe, in the heat of a temptation.

The Shield of Faith

The Roman shield was made of wood covered with leather and sometimes with metal. There were two types of shields. One was small and round; a soldier wore it on the arm for hand-to-hand combat. The other type was described as a door. The shield Paul was describing in Ephesians 6 was the large door model — it covered most of the soldier's body.

The Roman shields were designed to be drenched with water, which allowed them to withstand the fiery arrows of an enemy. A soldier needed only to kneel low and hold his shield over him, and he would be protected.

That's the way our faith operates. When the enemy fires thoughts into our minds, our faith quenches those thoughts.

Your faith is your most powerful weapon against the devil. It is the first line of your defense!

The devil sends the thought, *You've got to have this. It's important for your image and your witness.*

Faith puts out the thought with a response, "I will trust God to give me what He desires for me to have, and I will trust Him to help me use what He gives me to bring Him glory."

The devil sends the thought, *You should have this. You deserve this.*

Faith responds, "I will trust God to reward me as He sees fit."

The devil sends the thought, *You need*

to retaliate. You need to get even with that person who hurt you.

Faith responds, "I will trust God to retaliate on my behalf."

The devil sends the thought, *You'll always be sick. You'll never get well.*

Faith responds, "I will trust God to heal me in His timing — now or in eternity."

The devil sends the thought, *You will always be poor.*

Faith responds, "Rich or poor, I will trust God to provide for me all that I need."

Faith doesn't simply refer to things in the spirit, mind, and heart. Faith is intended to work in every area of your life — it relates to your physical well-being, your material and financial well-being, your relationships. You are to trust God for everything and in every circumstance.

The Bible refers to three degrees of faith: little, great, and perfect.

Little faith says, "God can do this."

Great faith says, "God will do this."

Perfect faith says, "It's as good as done."

The stronger your faith, the more you are able to say, "I will trust God to deal with this in His way and in His timing. I will trust God to deliver me, defend me, vindicate me, provide for me, and in the end, reward me for my faithfulness."

A Wall of Defense

There's another interesting thing about these door-sized shields used by the Roman army. When a line of soldiers stood shoulder to shoulder with these shields in front of them, they created a wall of defense. Soldiers crouching behind their linked-together shields could move forward in relative safety and advance to the front line of battle in unison. The critical factor was that they stay linked together without any breaks in the wall created by their shields.

How important this concept is for us as believers in Christ Jesus! When we band together, uniting our faith to believe God for a great advance of the gospel into a nation or among a tribal group or culture, we see tremendous results. The devil is forced to retreat!

In like manner, when a tough time comes to a church or group of believers, those who band together in their faith nearly always experience great strength to endure the persecution and withstand the enemy's effort to destroy or undermine their church's effectiveness in a community. They see an advance or enlargement of their ministry — perhaps not immediately, but eventually.

The underground church around the world knows this to be true, and we in the United States and other nations need to catch up with them in our understanding that God responds to our faith. God does not respond to need — if that were true, God would clear out every hospital and wipe out every evidence of poverty in an instant. Neither does God respond to our mournful pleading. God responds to the faith He sees in the hearts of men and women who are 100 percent committed to trusting Him in all situations, at all times, and for all things.

The great prayer of Jesus, "Not My will but Yours," is the prayer that establishes us in faith. The prayer, "I trust You to act in my best interests and to drive the enemy far from me and bring about something of eternal benefit," is the prayer of faith that moves mountains.

Faith is not about what we can do for God. Faith is about what God desires to do for us, in us, and around us. Faith is believing God to act out of His infinite power and wisdom on our behalf.

The devil's fiery darts are no match for this kind of faith.

The Helmet of Salvation

The apostle Paul admonished the Ephesians to "take the helmet of salvation" (Eph. 6:17).

As was true of the shield, Roman helmets were usually made of leather, sometimes with plates of metal at the temples and forehead. Battles in that time were often fought with clubs or pieces of chain as well as swords and daggers. A helmet protected the head from blows in hand-to-hand combat. Sometimes soldiers rode horses, and a helmet was especially important if a soldier fell from a horse.

To take the helmet of salvation means to remind ourselves that Jesus is our Savior, and that what He has done for us, He desires to do for others. It is to remind ourselves that we once were sinners and that by His grace, we are no longer in bondage to sin. It is to remind ourselves that the Holy Spirit is always with us to save us from the enemy.

Every believer who accepts Jesus Christ as Savior is saved from the judgment and eternal death of sin. Salvation is the experience of confessing sin, acknowledging that what Jesus did on the cross was the full sacrifice required by God for the punishment of sin, and receiving what Jesus did on one's behalf.

Once a person has accepted Jesus as Savior and is saved, he does not need to be saved again. The work that is done in that moment of acceptance of Christ is an eternal work of the Holy Spirit. The Holy Spirit immediately seals that spiritual decision and indwells the believer, and nothing anybody can do or say — including the person who is saved — can undo what the Holy Spirit has done. A person may fail to continue in his walk with the Lord — a person may fail to worship and serve Christ with his whole heart, and therefore, the person may be subject to chastisement and a loss of potential rewards in eternity — but the person cannot reverse a genuine spiritual birth.

Jesus is the Savior. His work in us is salvation. There is tremendous benefit in calling to our minds often the truth that Jesus, by His mercy and loving-kindness, died on a cross so that we might live free of sin and inherit an eternal home in heaven.

Nobody can monitor or govern your thinking but you. You govern what you will dwell on in your mind. You have the power to dismiss thoughts or to entertain thoughts.

And what is the most important thought to keep at the forefront of your thinking? It is the truth that *Jesus is my Savior.*

Now, what happens to you when this thought is your first thought at all times?

You have a keen awareness that you have been delivered from the bondage of sin. You have deep gratitude for your deliverance from sin and your ability to live a pure and God-pleasing life. You have a deep knowing that sin destroys health, relationships, finances, and the fulfillment of your purpose in this life. You have a deep understanding that certain things no longer fit you as a believer in Christ Jesus, and you have no desire to dabble with sin, toy with sin, or entertain sin in your life.

You also have deep compassion for other people who are in need of the Savior.

When you recall your salvation with thanksgiving for what God has done on your behalf, you find that you have a growing desire to see other people experience what you have experienced. You are quicker to witness to the truth of Jesus as Savior. You are quicker to give thanks and offer praise for your salvation. You are more eager to pray and intercede that others might come to know Him.

Ongoing Rescue

Salvation, in this passage in Ephesians, does not refer solely to a person's initial acceptance of Christ as Savior. This word for salvation refers also to God's ongoing rescuing and delivering power.

The helmet protects the head — the brain, the mind. As we discussed in an earlier chapter, the mind is the real spiritual battleground on which the enemy fights his strongest, dirtiest, bloodiest, and most important battles! We must protect our thought lives. We must trust God to save us, rescue us, and deliver us from the onslaught of messages that we encounter every day. We must remind ourselves continually that God desires to save us from all doubt and to deliver us from all lies.

Bumper stickers, television sets, people on the streets, advertising signs, and music blaring from radios and loudspeakers — all bombard us daily with messages that deny the saving power of God. The message of the world is, "You have to save yourself. It's up to you. You have to look out for number one."

God's Word declares just the opposite:

We trust in the living God, who is the Savior. (1 Tim. 4:10)

255

My defense is of God, who saves the upright in heart. (Ps. 7:10)

Blessed be the Lord,
Who daily loads us with benefits,
The God of our salvation!
Our God is the God of salvation;
And to God the Lord belong escapes
from death. (Ps. 68:19–20)

Christ . . . is the Savior of the body [the church]. (Eph. 5:23)

The truth is, you cannot save yourself. You cannot save yourself from sin. You cannot save yourself from all acts of terror, all temptations, or all accidents and sicknesses. God alone is your Savior.

There's another aspect of this that is critically important to the way you live your life every day.

People who do not believe that Jesus is their Savior and that God desires to save them from life's trials live with doubt and discouragement. They have no hope! They know they are limited in their own resources and ability. They know that bad things sometimes happen to good people. They know that trouble comes in unexpected ways in the least opportune times.

If you don't know today that Jesus is your Savior and that God desires to rescue you from the evil of this world, you can't possibly have an upbeat, positive, enthusiastic zest for living. In all likelihood, you are living at the edge of discouragement, despair, and disillusionment. You feel twinges of fear and doubt and anxiety at the unfolding of every negative news story and every idle piece of gossip circulating in your company or community.

But if you know that Jesus is your Savior and you are 100 percent convinced that God desires to rescue you from evil, you have a great capacity for hope. There's something better just ahead! God is in control, and His purposes are going to unfold for your benefit — both now and in eternity! Those who eagerly anticipate God's deliverance see God's miracles unfolding all around them. They actively receive God's outpoured blessings and use them to bring God glory.

Nobody can make you think, *God is in the process of saving me right now!* You have to choose to think that thought in every negative situation, in every troublesome moment, and in every painful and traumatic experience.

I heard the story about a young woman

who was mugged on a city street and was on the verge of being raped at knifepoint. She kept saying repeatedly to herself and to her assailant, "Jesus is my Savior. Jesus is my Savior. Jesus is my Savior." The man became so troubled by what she was saying that he eventually released her and ran from her.

Now, such a statement is not a magic formula to use in a time of trouble, but, friend, such a statement is a declaration of the truth! We do well to remind ourselves often, "Jesus is my Savior!" We do well to say to others, "Jesus is my Savior. He desires to be your Savior too."

The Sword of the Spirit

The third weapon that the apostle Paul admonished the Ephesians to "take up" was the "sword of the Spirit" (Eph. 6:17).

The Romans used a short sword that was designed for close hand-to-hand combat. It was only about eighteen inches long. The most effective sword was sharpened on both sides so that no matter which way it was wielded in the hand of the soldier, it had cutting power. The sword was not only a defensive weapon. It was a weapon of offense. In fact, the sword is the only piece of the armor described by Paul that is geared for both defense and offense. In that regard, it truly is two-sided — defending us against the devil and actively forcing the devil to retreat from us.

Paul clearly stated that the sword is the "sword of the Spirit" and that it is the "word of God." The specific Greek word for the "word of God" in this passage is *rhema* — which is a timely word of God applied to a particular situation by the power of the Holy Spirit.

The Holy Spirit is the One who inspired men of old to write the Scriptures. The Holy Spirit is the One who reminds us today of the Scriptures. Jesus said, "When He, the Spirit of truth, has come, He will guide you into all truth; for He will not speak on His own authority, but whatever He hears He will speak; and He will tell you things to come. He will glorify Me, for He will take of what is Mine and declare it to you" (John 16:13–14).

The written Word of God, when spoken aloud into a particular situation by the inspiration of the Holy Spirit and with the authority of the Holy Spirit, is a powerful, irreplaceable weapon against the devil. It is the weapon that puts the devil on the run.

It is the weapon that pushes back the forces of darkness that may seem overwhelming. The Bible is your most powerful weapon in defeating the devil.

To become adept at wielding the sword of the Spirit, the Word of God, you need to know God's Word and to be armed with an arsenal of verses that specifically refer to your particular weakness. How might you do this?

First, use a concordance, and look up every verse that relates to the temptation that seems to come to you most often. For example, if you repeatedly struggle with greed, or with feelings that you just gotta have particular items that you see as you pass a store window, you need to look up verses that deal with the wise use of money and good stewardship. You need to look up verses that talk about greed and about God's power to help you overcome greedy impulses.

If you have difficulty controlling what you eat, look up verses that deal with this impulse and that portray God's power in you to overcome this impulse.

If you have a problem with lusting after people sexually, look up verses that might counteract the thoughts the devil sends your way.

Then write out these verses. You may want to keep them handy. Read them often.

Over time, discipline your mind to memorize these verses. Repeat them to yourself frequently.

And then when a temptation comes your way, respond immediately by saying aloud a verse from your arsenal of Scriptures! Speak out God's Word. Let your ears hear what you have to say.

Hebrews 4:12 explains that "the word of God is living and powerful, and sharper than any two-edged sword, piercing even to the division of soul and spirit, and of joints and marrow, and is a discerner of the thoughts and intents of the heart." God's Word penetrates to the level of your thoughts and intents. It reveals your motivations, desires, and sins.

When you quote the Bible in times of temptation, two things happen.

First, you feel strength to stand and resist the devil. Your faith is quickened, your hope is renewed, and your mind and heart are put into a state of full readiness to act in a way that is pleasing to God. In speaking God's Word, you are doing something actively and positively that causes you to draw near to God, and God's promise is that if you "draw near to God . . . He will draw near to you" (James 4:8). Your mind will be sharpened. Your heart will be cleansed. Very positive things happen in you when you recite God's Word!

Second, the devil has to flee. James 4:7 urges you to "resist the devil and he will flee from you." There are no ifs, buts, or maybe's about that verse. When you speak God's Word, you activate your resistance, and the devil must flee from you. He must back off. He must cease his temptation. Certainly he may come again, but in that moment, he must leave.

The Three Work Together

Now take a look at the whole of these three pieces of armor that the apostle Paul told us to "take up."

When you activate your faith to believe that God will defend you and defeat the enemy on your behalf, you experience greater courage and confidence.

When you set your mind to look for, anticipate, eagerly expect, and openly receive God's saving power, you experience a heightened sense of hope. You live with renewed enthusiasm for the future — on this earth and in heaven.

When you pick up the Word of God and actively speak it to yourself and to the enemy, you experience a renewed awareness of the Holy Spirit alive and working in you and on your behalf.

When you are strong in faith, filled with hope, and keenly aware of the Holy Spirit's presence and power, you are not going to fall victim to the devil's fiery darts of temptation or crumble and wither under the devil's attacks! You are going to win the battle every time. You are going to see the truth of the situation, make the decisions that result in righteousness, and move into troubled areas of life with deep assurance that God is in control and His will shall be done.

The apostle Paul didn't just admonish us to be strong in the Lord — he told us how to be strong. He told us what it means to trust in the power of God's might. He told us what it takes to stand up to the tricks of the devil.

When we wrap ourselves in the identity of Christ Jesus as our Truth, our Righteousness, and our Peace and then arm ourselves with a mind-set that "God is my Savior in this situation; He is my hope, He is my Defender, He is my Victor; God is my ever-present Ally," we have the strength to stand against anything the devil may send our way!

Putting On Your Armor

Before you get out of bed in the morning, I encourage you to mentally and verbally put on these pieces of armor. Say aloud to the Lord:

Lord, by faith here's what I'm doing right now to prepare myself for the coming day. I'm putting on the belt of truth. I ask You to make it very clear to me what I am to accept into my life and what I am to reject. Help me to see clearly the motives of others as they deal with me and converse with me. Let me walk in Your truth, making decisions and choices according to Your plans and purposes for my life.

I am putting on the breastplate of righteousness. Guard my emotions today. Protect my heart. Help me to take into my life only the things that are pure, and nothing that is poison or polluting. Help me to live in integrity and to have a reputation based upon doing, saying, believing, thinking, and feeling the right things. Help me to live in right relationship with You every moment of this coming day.

I am putting on my spiritual boots. Help me to stand and walk in Your peace and to move forward in ways that bring Your peace and love to others. Help me to have the full confidence and assurance that come from knowing that I am filled with the peace that only You can give to those who are Your children. Help me to be a peacemaker. Show me where to walk and how to walk as You would walk.

I am picking up the shield of faith. Help me to trust You to be my Victor in every area of life today. Help me to trust You to defend me, provide for me, and keep me in safety every hour of this day.

I am putting on my helmet of salvation. Guard my mind today. Bring to my remembrance all that You have done for me as my Savior. Let me live in the hope and confidence that You are saving me — rescuing me and delivering me — from evil.

I am picking up my sword of the Spirit, the Word of God. Bring to my remembrance today the verses of the Bible that I have read and memorized, and help me to apply them to the situations and circumstances I will face. Let me use Your Word to bring Your light into the darkness of this world and to defeat the devil when he comes to tempt me.

Father, I want to be fully clothed with the identity of Jesus Christ today. I am in Christ. He is in me. Help me to fully realize and accept that He is my Truth, my Righteousness, my Peace, my Savior, the source of my faith, and the ever-present Lord of my life.

I want to bring glory to Your name today. I ask all of this in the name of Jesus. Amen.

The Armor Is Your Identity in Christ

Several times in this book I have referred to the statement, "Christ is in me, and I am in Christ." That message is at the heart of the Christian's life. When we put on the whole armor of God, we put on the fullness of the identity, "I in Christ, Christ in me."

The apostle Paul admonished, "Be strong in the Lord and in the power of His might" (Eph. 6:10). All of the pieces of spiritual armor — offensive and defensive — flow from this verse. We obviously do not put on real pieces of armor. Neither do we put on ideas or activities. When we put on the whole armor of God, we put on the nature of Christ Jesus. We put on His identity, embrace fully His lordship of us, and spiritually clothe ourselves from head to toe, inside and out, with His presence and power.

These pieces of armor are not signs of our spiritual power or authority. Rather, they are an acknowledgment of His power and authority. These pieces of armor are not about us or about what we can do to protect ourselves. No! They are about Christ Jesus and His power to protect us and do what He has promised to do on our behalf against all the forces of hell!

Putting on the whole armor of God is all about being "in Christ." It is a graphic way of reminding us who we are in Him.

In contrast to all of the devil's lies, Jesus stands as our Truth.

In contrast to all of the wickedness that the devil tempts us to do, Jesus stands as our Righteousness.

In contrast to the death and destruction that the devil seeks to foist on our lives, Jesus is our salvation.

In contrast to all fear, doubt, and anxiety, Jesus is our source of faith.

In contrast to all of the world's philosophies and ideas, Jesus is the Word of God.

When you put on the full armor of God, you say to the devil, "You have to go through Jesus to get to me! You may launch fiery darts against me. You may assault my mind with your temptations, doubts, fears, and lies. But you cannot defeat me. I am in Christ and He is in me, and there is nothing you can do to touch or destroy my security in Him. Christ Jesus is my all in all."

11

Standing Strong in Prayer

Have you ever heard the phrase "all dressed up with no place to go"?

That may be the way you feel after reading through the last two chapters on the three pieces of armor you are to have on and the three pieces of armor you are to take up.

What are you to do when you are fully clothed with the identity of Christ?

The first word of the apostle Paul was this: "Stand."

God's Word does not tell you to attack or to mount a massive charge against the devil. God's Word tells you to stand on the truth of what Jesus has already accomplished.

Defeating the devil is Jesus' part. Standing firm is your part!

Standing firm means refusing to give in to the devil's temptations, and refusing to give up on what God is seeking to do in you and through you.

In writing to the Ephesians, the apostle

Paul repeatedly used words and phrases of resistance: "be strong in the Lord," "stand against the wiles," "withstand in the evil day," "having done all, to stand," "stand therefore" (Eph. 6:10–18). A stance of resistance was also evident in the book of James: "Resist the devil and he will flee from you" (4:7). Peter wrote about the devil this way: "Be sober, be vigilant; because your adversary the devil walks about like a roaring lion, seeking whom he may devour. Resist him, steadfast in the faith" (1 Peter 5:8–9). The word for "resist" comes from the same root word in the Greek that means "stand firm."

To resist does not mean to debate or to argue against the devil. It doesn't even mean to openly rebuke or chastise the devil. To resist means simply to stand firm in your belief that Jesus is greater than the devil and that you are in relationship with Jesus!

The statement "Be strong in the Lord and in the power of His might" is a command. God does not command you to do things you cannot do! You can stand in strength. You can resist.

Too many people say, "I'm weak. I just can't stand up to this barrage of temptations. I just can't survive this horrible attack."

Yes, you can.

There is nothing weak or wavering about the person who stands fully clothed with the identity of Christ Jesus. In Christ, you have power, but that power is not of your own making or rooted in your personality, skills, talents, intellect, or physical body. Your power is the power of Christ in you.

There is nothing uncertain or lacking in the power of Jesus. He has all authority over creation, over mankind, and over the spiritual realm. His power is available to you because you are in Christ and He is in you in the form of the Holy Spirit.

Jesus Christ is the true source of any power you have over the devil. When you put on the whole armor of God, you put on His power. You must never attempt to stand against the devil in your own strength. If you attempt to stand up to or resist the devil in your humanity or individual power, you'll be defeated every time.

But before you become discouraged or fearful, remember this eternal truth: Christ Jesus has defeated the devil. The power of God so far exceeds that of the devil that there is no possible comparison. And Christ Jesus gives you His spiritual authority, strength, and power the instant you accept Him as your Savior.

From the moment that you accepted Jesus as your Savior, God the Holy Spirit came to indwell you. He is living inside you. And the Bible clearly states that the Holy Spirit in you has greater power than the devil (1 John 4:4).

Can you truly stand against anything the devil throws at you?

Again I say, "Yes, you can."

The Power of Prayer

What do we do as we "stand"?

We pray.

I have faced major challenges in my life — physical, emotional, and relationship challenges. People have asked me at the height of some of those situations, "Why are you so upbeat? Aren't you concerned?"

Of course, I was concerned. At times I was in great pain. But above all, I have confidence in my life that God is in control! God is in charge of my life, and He will help me through all things in a way that brings eternal benefit to me and glory to Him! My relationship with God is the source of my strength. And that relationship is rooted and grounded in prayer.

How will you get the strength of the

living God operative in your life? How will you release it? Only through prayer! It is through prayer that we move into the offensive as we battle the enemy who assails us.

The apostle Paul left no doubt that everything we do to fully arm ourselves in the strength of the Lord and the power of His might is a prelude to this: "Praying always with all prayer and supplication in the Spirit, being watchful to this end with all perseverance and supplication for all the saints" (Eph. 6:18).

One of the main reasons that so many believers in Christ are weak is that they do not pray when the devil attacks them.

Prayer is not a piece of spiritual armor against the devil. Prayer is what we do once we are clothed in the armor that is the identity of Jesus.

At the Heart of Relationship

Through prayer, we relate to God and build a relationship with Him.

God's goal is to establish and develop an ever-deepening relationship with us. He desires to reveal Himself to us and to give us more and more of His presence and power to bring about His plans and purposes on this earth.

The devil's goal is to keep us from establishing a relationship with God and, if he fails at that, to keep us from growing in the Lord and developing a deeper and deeper relationship with God. He desires to keep us from experiencing God in our lives — to keep us from having God's presence and power actively at work in us to accomplish God's goals for mankind.

Plain and simple — God wants you and desires you and seeks to relate to you. The devil wants to destroy you and keep you from the embrace of God's love, mercy, and forgiveness.

A woman once said to me, "The strongest attacks of the devil that I experience seem to come when I'm praying. Is there something wrong with the way I'm praying?"

I said, "No, there's something very right about the way you're praying!"

The devil will do his utmost to distract us while we pray because he knows the effectiveness of a righteous person who is praying with faith. He'll send little thoughts into our minds to get us off track — it might be the grocery list, a little thought of anxiety about a particular person or situation, or the image of something we think we should be doing rather than praying.

When we aren't praying, the devil will do what he can to keep us from praying. He tells us that we are too busy to pray, that prayer isn't all that important, that we aren't very effective in our prayers, and that prayer is just talking to ourselves, not God.

Satan says, "You don't need to pray about this."

Satan says, "You shouldn't bother God with such a minor request."

Satan says, "You surely shouldn't expect God to answer that request."

Satan says, "You don't have time to pray."

Satan says, "The Bible doesn't really mean 'pray all the time.' "

The devil is a liar about prayer!

The devil doesn't want you to trust God in all situations. He doesn't want you to pray and trust God for blessings in your life. He doesn't want you to praise God and voice thanks to God. He doesn't want you to petition God to bring about what God desires to do in your life or the lives of others you love. The devil knows far better than most human beings just how potent prayer is and how directly prayer is related to his destruction!

The devil knows that we are the most

vulnerable to his attack when we don't pray.

What Happens When We Don't Pray

Satan has a very specific strategy when it comes to your prayer life. His strategy involves four stages:

Stage #1: Prayerlessness. Satan will seek to keep you very busy or distracted to the point that you do not pray, you do not voice your thanksgiving to God, and you do not praise God's name.

When you don't pray, you will become more anxious about things, more concerned about things that you cannot change, and more fearful of things, some of which are unknown. The result is that you become a burden bearer.

Stage #2: Burden bearing. The person who doesn't pray can feel as if he were carrying the weight of the world. He feels responsible for everything, and because such a responsibility is overwhelming, many people swing over and take the exact opposite approach and claim that they aren't responsible for anything. In truth, they feel a weight in their souls. The person who bears burdens in his own strength has a heavy heart.

Stage #3: Weariness. The person with a heavy heart experiences great weariness. Are you aware that people who live with constant needs, frustrations, or worries rarely have very much energy? They can be so overwhelmed by the sorrows, problems, and anxieties of their lives that they become almost paralyzed — they have no energy to exert on spreading the gospel, no energy to spend on helping others in need, and no energy to get up, get dressed, and get to church. They often feel too weary to read their Bibles or pray!

Stage #4: Weakness. When a person becomes discouraged and weary — spiritually, emotionally, or physically — he is in a state of weakness. And the weaker a person becomes, the more he will focus on himself, his needs, and his failures or "lack" in some area of life.

The weak animal in the wild is always most vulnerable to predators, and the same is true for us as human beings when it comes to the devil. The weaker and more self-focused we become on our unmet needs and unfulfilled desires, the more we drop our guard against the devil.

A person who is strong in prayer does

not take on the weight of the world. He trusts God to take care of every aspect of life and to take care of the world as a whole.

A person who is strong in praise has great joy, and that joy in turn produces great spiritual strength. God's Word declares, "The joy of the LORD is your strength" (Neh. 8:10). The person who prays has renewed energy and a zest for living. Such a person feels strong and is eager to take on life's challenges.

If you could name one thing Satan hates above all else, it is this: believers in Christ Jesus who know how to talk to the Father and trust the Father and claim the promises of the Father. Persevering prayer, built on a foundation of faith, crushes the power of the devil.

When we don't pray, however, we set ourselves up to be defeated by the devil.

Don't leave your home in the morning . . .

Don't do your job . . .

Don't go to sleep at night . . . without talking to the Lord.

Insights into Effective Prayer

Prayer is serious communication with your heavenly Father. Your prayers are the essential building blocks of your relationship with God. Quick prayers work only if you are "prayed up." Spend time in prayer. Get to know your heavenly Father. Don't just talk to God. Listen to God. Receive His wisdom into your life. Let Him reveal Himself to you and express His love to you.

Get down on your knees. Certainly you can pray in any position, but I believe there is something very important about bowing our knees before our heavenly Father. It is an act of submission and reliance upon Him. You wouldn't stand in the presence of almighty God if He walked into the room where you are right now. You would fall on your face before Him. You would bend your knee. The bended knee expresses a humbling of the body and, in turn, a humbling of the soul — it is a sign to yourself that you acknowledge dependence upon God.

Note again what the apostle Paul wrote to the Ephesians: "Praying always with all prayer and supplication in the Spirit, being watchful to this end with all perseverance and supplication for all the saints — and for me, that utterance may be given to me, that I may open my mouth boldly to make known the mystery of the gospel" (Eph. 6:18–19).

Paul used the word *always*. That refers to repeated and continual prayer.

We are to pray with all prayer. The word for *prayer* here refers to general praise, thanksgiving, and intercession. This form of prayer is focused on the general goodness of God, the greatness of God, the excellence of God, the glory of God. It is prayer that thanks God for every blessing, praises God for every one of His attributes, and offers petitions that God's purposes on this earth might be accomplished just as Jesus prayed: "On earth as in heaven."

We are to pray with all petition. The word for *prayer* here refers to the voicing of a particular request or prayer that addresses a specific need. It is prayer that asks God to do something in a particular life, situation, or circumstance. Jesus said, "Ask anything in My name that brings glory to the Father and I will do it." (See John 14:13; 15:16.) Petitioning is asking God to do specific things that you perceive will advance His kingdom on this earth and bring glory to God.

Petitioning is not saying a blanket "Bless me" or "Bless them." It is asking for something very specific and well defined. It may be asking for an infusion of wisdom or discernment. It may be asking for healing or financial provision. It may be asking for protection or the meeting of a particular emotional need.

We are to pray at all times. In admonishing the Ephesians to pray always, the apostle Paul did not mean that they were to be talking all the time. Rather, he meant that they were to be in an attitude of prayer at all times so that they were quick to hear, quick to request, and quick to offer praise and thanksgiving. In writing to the Thessalonian church, Paul also wrote, "Pray without ceasing" (1 Thess. 5:17).

Praying at all times means that we live with a "God consciousness" — we are aware of His presence with us at all times and in all circumstances. It means that we always factor God into every relationship, every conversation, and every experience.

To pray always means to see life through a "God filter" — we see situations through God's eyes and always see Him in relationship to us. We acknowledge that God is vitally concerned and involved with everything that concerns or involves us. We ask ourselves frequently, *What would God say about this? What is God doing? What aspect of God's power or presence is needed in this situation?*

To pray always means to open a connection with God — just as if we were calling Him on a telephone — and then never breaking that connection or never hanging up. It means to have the line always open to speak to God or hear from God.

You might say, "Well, I can't think about God all the time."

Let me ask you, "What do you find incompatible with thoughts of God? What is it that you can't pray about? What is it that you can't praise God for or thank God for?" If something comes to your mind, friend, that is the very thing you need to pray to God about! If there's something in your life that you don't want God involved in, that something is very likely sin.

Listen for God to Speak to You

Trust God to speak to you about everything in your life. Pay attention when He does speak!

God is concerned about even little things in your life. I usually have a very full schedule every day, and I often go to various places in a given day to do different things. One thing I've learned to do before I leave my house in the morning is to ask the Lord, "Do I have everything I need today?" Sometimes I get a green light, and I leave the house with confidence that I'm prepared to take on all the challenges ahead. Sometimes I have a little nudge in my spirit that I need to take something from my files or remember to do something before I leave the house. One Sunday morning I neglected to heed one of these little nudges, and I showed up at church without my Bible — the one that I had marked for that morning's sermon!

Ask the Lord frequently, "Lord, what do You want to tell me? What do You want to show me? What do You want to reveal to me about this person, this situation, this opportunity, this problem, this relationship?"

Then listen to and heed what the Lord says!

Pray About Everything

The Lord has a plan and specific direction for every opportunity, challenge, responsibility, or decision in your life. God desires to be part of every aspect of every day! Although I encouraged you to pray at length and to pray on your knees, you should also feel free to pray in any place while doing virtually anything. You can pray

- while driving your car. That's a good place to pray, especially given today's angry drivers and overcrowded freeways!
- while working in your office.
- while standing at the ironing board.
- while preparing dinner.
- while walking on a treadmill or walking around the block.
- while pulling weeds in the flower bed.
- while doing anything!

Pray and Intercede in the Spirit

Paul admonished the Ephesians to pray "in the Spirit." This does not refer to praying in tongues or in a spiritual language. Praying in the Spirit means to pray under the guidance of the Holy Spirit. It means to be sensitive to His promptings about what to pray, how to pray, and for whom to pray. It means to obey His promptings to speak or act in specific ways at specific times.

At times we feel a burden to pray for a person or situation, but we don't know what to pray. It is then that we need to say to the Holy Spirit, "Show me how to pray. Show me what You desire to do."

Praying in the Spirit means that we put ourselves spiritually in a position to be in full agreement with the Spirit about a specific petition. It means saying, "Lord, I don't know how to pray about this. Lord, I don't know what to ask for or what to say. But, Lord, I want what You want. I want to pray what You want me to pray. I want to pray Your best into my life or the life of another person. I want to live in obedience to Your will for my life and to see others live in obedience and experience the fullness of Your approval on their lives. Show me how I ought to pray!"

Pray anytime a person comes to your mind in a strong, sudden, or special way.

Pray about those situations that you sense may be just beyond the immediate horizon of your life or their lives.

The more you pray, the more you are going to understand what you are praying for. I have seen this in my life and in the lives of a number of godly intercessors I know. A godly intercessor may very well know some things about the person he is praying for that the person may not even know about himself! Why? Because God has revealed those things to the intercessor so he can pray on the person's behalf.

As you pray for other people, don't pray in a critical way. Pray for God's best in their lives. Pray for God to redeem them, save them, change them, and then bless them. That kind of prayer will open you up to experiencing greater forgiveness and blessings in your life.

Do you love some individuals enough to intercede for them and to pray for them with God's love flowing freely in your spirit?

Pray with Faith

We are always to pray with unwavering faith that God not only will hear our prayers but also will answer them, in His timing, with His methods, and always for His glory and our eternal benefit. You can count on it!

As you pray in the face of a spiritual attack, set your mind on the vastness of God's power. See Him for the mighty God He is! God created all things — the heavens and the earth. He moves mountains and calms seas. He has power over death. He gives us an eternal home in heaven. In the face of fear, He gives us boldness. Paul wrote to Timothy: "God has not given us a spirit of fear, but of power and of love and of a sound mind" (2 Tim. 1:7).

The Many Benefits of Praying

There are countless other benefits to your prayers:

- Your understanding of the Word of God is in direct proportion to your prayers.
- Your holiness and righteousness are directly related to your prayers.
- Your fruitfulness and usefulness to God are directly related to your prayers.

In the face of spiritual attack, let me remind you of these three specific benefits of prayer: greater discernment, greater awareness of sin that you need to confess, and greater energy and strength.

Discernment

Prayer gives us greater discernment. It is in prayer and as the result of prayer that we are able to see what others don't see. We especially are able to see the lies of the devil for what they are.

Prayer is also our foremost way of

hearing God speak in our hearts to give us a warning or forewarning of something — it may be something little or big. We need to pay attention to the still, small voice of God warning us.

A couple of years ago the Lord gave me very clear warning of a problem that was going to come my way. I have to admit, I wasn't fully aware of the specifics of what He was telling me, but I did know that this message from the Lord was troubling. I knew that this message had come to me on three different occasions; therefore, it involved something important, and I was to recognize a trick of the enemy against me.

Then the attack came. I was surprised, and yet I wasn't surprised. I was surprised in the moment, but I wasn't surprised as I reflected later about the situation. In the moment, I was able to withstand the attack and maintain a godly stance. Upon reflection, I recognized God's warning, and I acted immediately to put some safeguards into my life so I would not be vulnerable to such an attack in the future.

But what if I wasn't steeped in prayer? What if I hadn't experienced God's warning? I may very easily have thought, *Well, that isn't really an attack of the devil. That's just a silly person acting foolishly toward me.* I could have thought, *You know, if you look at that from one perspective, it could be taken as a compliment.* And if I had gone down that path and allowed subsequent or similar attacks — perhaps even inviting them by my lack of establishing a defense against them — I could very well have suffered a major blow to my integrity and reputation.

A Self-Awareness of Sin

One of the most difficult things for any person to see clearly is his own sin.

God does not reveal to us our sin so that we feel condemned by and doomed in our sin — rather, so that we can confess it, repent of it, and be free of it!

The good news for each one of us is that in prayer, God reveals to us our areas of weakness, not just in personality or spirit or emotional makeup. God will reveal to us areas in our finances, marriages, friendships, businesses or careers, and ministries that need to be strengthened or renewed. God will reveal to us ways to protect ourselves and still be effective and fully functional.

It is in prayer that you are in the best position for the Holy Spirit to prick your conscience about a particular sin or weakness that God desires for you to address.

It is in prayer that you begin to experience very subtle feelings that reveal the real desires of your heart. Sometimes the subtle feelings are the first insight that you are harboring anger, unforgiveness, or bitterness.

It is in prayer that God gives flashes of insight into His Word and into His plans and purposes for you in any given day.

Prayer puts you into a position where God can guide you very gently. Prayer confirms to your heart that God is guarding you closely and is present with you always.

Renewed Strength and Energy
Paul wrote to the Romans,

The Spirit also *helps in our weaknesses*. For we do not know what we should pray for as we ought, but the Spirit Himself makes intercession for us with groanings which cannot be uttered. Now He who searches the hearts knows what the mind of the Spirit is, because He makes intercession for the saints according to the will of God. (Rom. 8:26–27, italics added for emphasis)

When you trust God in prayer, you receive help in weakness. You become strong spiritually — nothing other than prayer produces this type of spiritual strength!

Prayer produces God's divine energy in you. It is the means by which God pours His power into your life so that you have the strength — mental, emotional, physical, and spiritual — to do everything God has prepared for you and called you to do.

Watch and Persevere

The apostle Paul's final two words to the Ephesians about their prayer life were these: *watch* and *persevere*. Jesus said in the Garden of Gethsemane, "Watch and pray." Be alert to what is happening around you! He wanted His disciples to be on the alert and, even more important, to see how He was facing the greatest hour of emotional need in His life.

Choose to learn from God.

The apostle Paul wrote that they were to be "watchful" (Eph. 6:18). We are called to be alert in our prayers. We are to be wide awake about situations in which we find ourselves and aware of the people around us.

He wrote that they were to pray "with all perseverance" (Eph. 6:18). To persevere means to pray with a steadfast intensity of faith. To persevere means to live in a state of constant readiness to receive God's answer and act on it.

To persevere means to pray as long as it takes for the answer to come — it means that we don't quit until the answer appears!

Simply stated, to persevere means to pray

- with a steadfastness of faith
- with an intensity of desire
- with readiness to receive God's instructions and act on them immediately
- with a commitment to continuing in prayer until we receive God's answer

I started to get up one day from a time of prayer, but God said, "Not yet." I immediately got back down on my knees. There was something more that I needed to see or something more that I needed to pray.

If you feel that you have hit a brick wall in your praying, that's precisely the time to keep praying. That's the very point at which you must not stop.

Perseverance means being available for God to speak to you. Don't rush in and say, "Do You have anything to say to me?" Often the Lord will wait for you to have a quiet heart, a calm spirit, an expectant attitude before He will reveal to you His desire or His plan.

Perseverance also means that you make a commitment to spend time every day with the Lord and that you are quick to talk to God about anything, anybody, and any circumstance, anywhere, and at any time. You pray not only because it is the right thing to do but also because it is the most powerful thing you can do. You pray with the full expectancy that God will use your prayers to change circumstances and to change lives. You pray with the full expectancy that God will empower you to resist Satan's attacks!

12

Protecting Your Family

Many years ago now, a father said to me, "Dr. Stanley, I want a godly family more than anything. But things are so bad right now, I don't even know where to start in helping my family to be restored."

He went on to tell me that his company asked him to take an assignment overseas. He had agreed to the new role because it meant a significant increase in salary and the company had told him that he'd be gone only two years. The company agreed to move his family to the new location or to give him a week off every three months to travel home. He talked over the position with his wife and children, and they all agreed that it was a good opportunity for him and that he should take the position. They further agreed that they wanted him to come home every three months so the children could stay in their schools and they could continue to live in their home and be part of the community and church they had grown to love.

The new position was filled with a great deal of stress. The work hours were long, and the demands were intense. The job was in a dangerous area of the world, and the man found that when he did go back to his apartment, he had trouble sleeping. He felt insecure, and the more he lay awake wondering about each sound outside, the more his mind mulled over the difficulties of the job assignment and the more his heart missed his wife and children. He began to take sleeping pills to help him sleep at night, and in the end, he became addicted to them as well as to heavy-duty pain medications he had started taking for the headaches he was having as a result of the stress and lack of sleep.

"It was a bad cycle of stress and no sleep and too many pills," he said.

Back home, his wife was lonely, and the more she withdrew into herself, the less she was able to comfort her children or discipline them. She, too, fell victim to stress. She began to take tranquilizers and then to overmedicate herself. By the end of the first year, this man and his wife were addicted to different kinds of pills!

The teenage children didn't handle the stress and tension of Dad being gone literally and Mom being gone emotionally. The teenage girl began to hang out with a group of young people who were ungodly, and she soon found herself pregnant. Her younger brother was angry at the whole situation and ran away from home to live with his grandparents on their farm. He wanted nothing to do with his father, his mother, or his pregnant sister.

The man decided to tell his company that he could no longer stay overseas, and the company, in turn, told him that he no longer had a job. He returned to his family desperate to find a job to support them, but the only job he could find meant that the family needed to move. The move was difficult on everybody, and they ended up in a new city angry with one another, sad and confused about how to put together a new life, addicted to chemicals, and coping with the approaching arrival of a baby in their midst.

"The devil has me and my family," this man said. "I don't know what to do. Is there any hope for us?"

I assured this man that God desired to help him and would help him. I outlined to him what I'm going to share with you. But I also recognized, even as he told me his story, that his family situation was not all that different from thousands of families across our nation. The details and circumstances might be different, but the overall condition was the same. Tens of millions of families are under attack these days.

Let me address three things with you. First, how Satan gets into a family. Second, how we can turn things around with God's help. And third, what we can do to protect our families against his attacks.

How Satan Invades a Family

Satan gets into a family by one of two methods. He may invade a family by direct assault — destroying the possessions of a family or attacking the health of a family member. The family immediately is under intense stress caused by external circumstances over which the family members had no control. Unless they guard themselves against the devil and resist him with their faith and the Word of God, they likely are to become confused, wounded, and divided.

A woman told me about two families in her hometown who experienced the loss of their homes through a sweeping forest fire that engulfed their mountain community. One family pulled together in faith, crying out to God for His help and encouraging one another with the Word of God. The other family began blaming God for what happened to them. That was accompanied by nonstop bickering and fighting about what to do, where to go, and who should be in charge of what. The family that pulled together as a unified family trusting in God had their home rebuilt and their life restored within eight months. The family that blamed God and lived in anger was still living in a rented apartment two years after the loss of the home. The parents were on the brink of divorce, and their children were angry and rebellious.

A tragic circumstance does not need to pull a family apart. It can bring a family together. The result will depend on how the family members respond spiritually to what has happened to them, and out of their spiritual response will come an emotional response that will make the family stronger or weaker.

At times the devil does not use a direct assault against a family's health or material possessions, but the devil will use an indirect tactic. He will tempt one member of the family to sin, and he usually begins with the father. If the devil can get a father to sin, he is well on his way to enslaving the entire family.

The father bears the final responsibility for the well-being of his family. If he allows pornographic literature into the home, allows the viewing of television violence or videos loaded with graphic sexual scenes, or allows certain chemicals to be stocked in his refrigerator or cabinets, he opens the door to sin.

One young man told me that his family had stopped going to church when his dad took up golf. He said, "Dad started playing golf on Sundays, and Mom gave up trying to get us kids ready for church on her own. There wasn't much she could say to my brother and me to convince us we needed to go to church. I opted to sleep in. My brother opted to learn to play golf so he could spend Sunday mornings with Dad."

The father, of course, is not the only person to be the focus of the devil's attack. I heard about a woman who abandoned her two junior-high-age children. She rented an apartment a few blocks from the family home and told her husband and children that she "needed her space" in order to "find herself" and "fulfill her potential." This wife and mother had bought into a lie of the devil that God's purposes for her would be better fulfilled outside the family He had given to her. I can only imagine the anger, hurt, and frustration of those children as they enter their high school years trying to sort out why their mother rejected them. They could easily become bitter that she left them to deal with life's issues on their own.

At times, a child might be attacked. The devil certainly doesn't wait to attack a person at age twenty if he can attack that person at a younger age. A child might get into drugs, be enticed to participate in gang activity, or be exposed to all kinds of sinful activities.

We must recognize that the sin of one person in a family affects the whole family — spiritually, emotionally, and perhaps materially, financially, and physically. Every member of the family is affected, even if a member of the family is off at college, in the military overseas, or married and with a family of his own. There's no such thing as a private, personal sin. Sin affects everybody close to the person who is sinning — including friends, fellow church members, neighbors, and co-workers.

Bringing Deliverance to the Family

There are several vital steps to bringing deliverance to any person trapped by sin as well as to a family enslaved by sin.

Recognize Your Position in Christ

First, you must recognize the position that you have in Christ. The believers in the family must openly recognize and acknowledge their position in Christ. You must openly profess that you belong to Christ Jesus and that He lives in you and is with you constantly by the power of His Holy Spirit. Acknowledge God's presence in your life, and recognize that He alone can deliver you from the enemy.

There may be a step you need to take as part of recognizing that you are in Christ and Christ is in you, even in the midst of your turmoil or tragedy. If you as a godly member of the family have sinned — by what you may have done or not done, by taking wrong, ill-advised action or by living in denial, by saying things that were hurtful or by not saying what would have been helpful — you need to face up to that sin, confess it to God, and receive His forgiveness for your part in contributing to

301

the sin of the ungodly family member.

This is not to say that you are to blame for the sin of the other person. That person's choice is his choice. He has free will to make decisions, and you are not responsible for the ungodly adult's willful choices and decisions. You are not responsible for situations in which ungodly people attacked your children — no parent is fully able to protect a child at all times and in all circumstances. But you may be responsible for failing in some way to create a loving environment; to warn or teach your children about certain substances, people, or activities; or to safeguard yourself and your family in some way. If anything comes to your mind with the accusation, *I could have done something and I didn't,* take that issue to God and ask for His forgiveness and cleansing from guilt.

Accept and receive God's forgiveness so that you can take a bold stand: "I am in Christ and Christ is in me. I will not back away from doing what is right before God. I will rely on the Holy Spirit daily to direct me, empower me, and give me His wisdom."

Do What You Know Is Godly
The second step in bringing deliverance

to your family — and to yourself if you are the person used by the devil to bring destruction to your family — is to begin to do and continue to do what you know to be right before God.

A man told me not long ago that when he made a new commitment to follow the Lord, he knew he needed to do five things: stop watching violent videos, go to an anger management class, attend church every Sunday morning and every Wednesday evening (which were the only times his church met), get involved in a Sunday school class, and quit drinking.

"How did you know that those were the specific things you needed to do?" I asked.

"God told me that those were the things I needed to start doing to build discipline in my life and to get the wisdom I needed. He added two more things a month later," he said.

"What were they?"

"God made it very plain that I needed to discipline myself to read my Bible at least twenty minutes a day and to pray at least ten minutes a day — mostly praising Him and listening to Him after I had read the Bible."

"Are you still doing those things?"

"I haven't seen a violent video or had a

drink in five years," he replied. "I took the anger management class and learned a lot. Going to church and Sunday school is now automatic — I don't even think about doing anything else on Sunday mornings or Wednesday evenings."

"What about the reading and praying?"

"I read my Bible and pray every day," he said, "but usually not for a half hour total time."

I must admit that I was surprised when he added, "Reading the Bible and praying have become so important to me that I usually spend an hour in the Word and on my knees."

"And how's your relationship with the Lord?" I asked.

His eyes filled with tears. "I can't put it into words," he finally said. "There's nothing more valuable to me than my relationship with Jesus."

I don't know what God will tell you specifically that you need to do, but I do know that it is always God's will that you read your Bible and pray every day, and that you get involved with a church and attend regularly. I also believe He will lead you to get involved in some form of ministry to others — perhaps within a church or perhaps witnessing to people or serving in some form of outreach ministry. Believers have followed these basic Christian disciplines since the very beginning of the church, and there is no substitute for them.

These disciplines will not only establish and ground you in God's Word and in your relationship with the Lord, but they will also bring about a change in the way you relate to your family members as you apply God's Word to your daily life. God desires for His Word to change us — to renew our minds, change our habits, strengthen our self-control, expand our ability to express love, renew our willingness to forgive and to show mercy, and enlarge our capacity for joy, patience, and kindness. God's Word, prayer, and a daily reliance upon the Holy Spirit work together in us to produce godly character.

Your family may not immediately join you in these disciplines, but you need to establish these disciplines for yourself, regardless of what your family members say or do. Even if they ridicule you, continue to do what you know are the right things to do in your walk with the Lord. I strongly believe that the more other family members see you following Christ in these practical, daily ways, they will be convicted that they need to adopt these disciplines as well.

As much as it is in your power to do so, cleanse your home of all ungodly objects or practices. If you are a parent, recognize that you have the authority over what is brought into your home. You have the authority to control what is read, viewed, listened to, or consumed. As long as you bear responsibility for a child — not only legally and financially, but as the parent of a child under your influence in your home — you have the authority over what occurs in your home.

You may need to clear out your refrigerator or cupboards, remove some things from your bookshelves, CD racks, and video or DVD storage areas, take down some posters, or do away with some artifacts. Ask God to reveal to you anything you need to cleanse from your home.

Pray for Your Family

Begin to pray in a concerted way for yourself and for your family members who are involved in sinful behaviors. Pray in these ways:

Pray in the name of Jesus. The Lord has given us His name to use. Jesus said to His disciples, "Whatever you ask in My name, that I will do, that the Father may be glorified in the Son. If you ask anything in My name, I will do it" (John 14:13–14).

To pray in the name of Jesus is not simply to say "in Jesus' name" at the end of a prayer. To pray in the name of Jesus is to pray what Jesus would pray on your behalf. It is to pray with an awareness of what God has promised to you, what is rightfully yours as a child of God, and what God has said He desires for you.

Plead the blood of Jesus over your lives. Revelation 12:11 tells us that the saints in heaven are those who "overcame him [the devil] by the blood of the Lamb and by the word of their testimony." To plead the blood of Jesus over your life and the lives of your family members is to come before the Lord and declare,

You, Lord Jesus, died for our sins so that we might be in relationship with God the Father. Your shed blood cleanses us from all sin. I ask You to cleanse me and my family from all unrighteousness. I ask You to protect us from evil, to redeem us, and to use us totally for Your purposes. I claim for myself and my family members the full provision of Your shed blood on our behalf — the full provision of Your saving, healing, delivering, cleansing, and renewing power!

In praying this way, you are reminding yourself in a powerful way of all that is rightfully yours as a result of Jesus' death on the cross on your behalf. You are declaring over your life what He purchased for you through His death and resurrection.

Pray the Word of God. Throughout the Word of God, we find numerous examples of the people of God reciting the Word of God as part of their prayers and praises. Openly declare to the Lord what you know to be true about Him, about your relationship with Him, about your utter dependence upon Him, and about His promises to you. Quote the Bible back to God, saying,

Lord, You say this in Your Word. I believe it. Help me to apply this to my life. Help me to receive the fullness of all that You have for me and for my family. What You have said, I profess to be true for me and for my family. Help us to be people who not only know the Word, but live out the Word in this world.

Pray with unwavering faith. The Bible tells us that we must pray with unwavering faith — without doubt, firmly believing that God will be true to His Word and that He will be faithful in His relationship with us. To pray with faith is to believe that the Lord who has begun a good work in us will continue that work until it is completed! (See James 1:6–8 and Philippians 1:6.)

Ask daily for the help of the Holy Spirit. Never assume that you can do it all or bring about the healing of yourself or your family members by your own strength, prayers, or faith. Ask daily for the help of the Holy Spirit. Voice your reliance upon Him to do His work in you, through you, and all around you. Submit your will to His will as you pray, "Not what I want, but what You want."

Be Bold in Your Testimony About Jesus

Your testimony is not based upon what you believe, what you have done, or what you are doing. Your testimony is based upon who Jesus is in your life, what He has done on your behalf, and what He desires to do in you, in your family, and through you and your family to others in your community.

When you hear a lie being told by a family member, speak the truth of God's Word.

When you hear statements of doubt about God's love or about God's provision, speak the truth of God's Word.

When you hear a family member take the Lord's name in vain, speak the truth about who Jesus is, who God is, and who the Holy Spirit is.

Don't allow yourself to become comfortable with "just a little sin" in your family. A little arsenic spoils a plate of food — a little cyanide poisons a large body of water. Sin is deadly. It pollutes and infects and destroys. Don't develop a tolerance for any amount of it in your life or in the lives of loved ones.

If you allow yourself to become comfortable with sin, you soon will begin to defend the presence of sin — to justify it and to give place to it. Deal with those issues that underlie a person's willingness to commit sin or to act in rebellion.

Protecting Yourself and Your Family

All of the things I have admonished you to do in the preceding section also apply to your protection of your family against sin:

- Openly profess your position in Christ Jesus. Praise the Lord often, and acknowledge His love, provision, and protection of you. Profess your position in Christ, thanking Him for saving you, delivering you from evil, and working all things together for your good.
- Do what you know is right before God. Establish disciplines that involve all family members — individually or collectively — and develop a pattern of encouraging one another in sustaining those disciplines.
- Pray for your family and with your family. Let your family members hear you call their names to the Lord in prayer.
- Be bold in your testimony about who Jesus is in your family and who He is in your personal life.

In addition to these things, I strongly encourage you to create what the Bible refers to as a "hedge" of protection around your family. A hedge is like a fence — it protects what is within it and keeps predators and thieves outside. (See Job 1:10.)

Specifically ask the Lord to send His angels to guard your family and to protect each member of your family each day. I encourage you to memorize Psalm 34. This psalm is filled with verses that you can pray over your family members each day.

Throughout any given day, as a family member comes to mind, praise God for that person and pray for God's best in his life.

"But," you may say, "what should I pray when I don't know anything specific to pray?"

You can always pray that a person will

- have the right attitude
- make the right choices and decisions
- get involved in the right activities
- associate with the right people, which has nothing to do with social status but everything to do with what is righteous and godly before the Lord
- say what is right, especially what is pleasing to the Lord

I strongly recommend that you pray Colossians 1:9–14. This prayer is God's Word! As God's Word, it expresses fully what God desires to do in our lives and the lives of those we love. It encapsulates precisely the will of God so we can pray God's will with boldness and faith. Read through this prayer slowly, pausing to insert your name or the name of a loved one periodically into the phrases and sentences of this prayer:

Since the day we heard it, [we] do not cease to pray for you, and to ask that you may be filled with the knowledge of His will in all wisdom and spiritual understanding; that you may walk worthy of the Lord, fully pleasing Him, being fruitful in every good work and increasing in the knowledge of God; strengthened with all might, according to His glorious power, for all patience and longsuffering with joy; giving thanks to the Father who has qualified us to be partakers of the inheritance of the saints in the light. He has delivered us from the power of darkness and conveyed us into the kingdom of the Son of His love, in whom we have redemption through His blood, the forgiveness of sins.

What a wealth of encouragement, love, and wisdom is in this prayer! God tells us very directly that He desires to give us these petitions of our hearts:

- God desires that we be filled with the knowledge of His will in all wisdom and spiritual understanding.
- God desires that we walk worthy of the Lord, fully pleasing Him.
- God desires that we be fruitful in every good work.
- God desires that we know Him better every day.
- God desires that we be strengthened with all might, according to the glorious power of the Holy Spirit at work in us.
- God desires that we have patience and be longsuffering with others, and have these attitudes and behaviors with joy in our hearts.
- God desires that we give thanks always to Him for our salvation.
- God desires that we be ever mindful that we have been delivered from the power of darkness — the enemy of our souls — and that we have been redeemed by the blood of Jesus.
- God desires that we live in an ongoing state of forgiveness, frequently confessing our faults to God and being forgiven of our sins so that we might

walk in purity and a continual new-
ness of life.

When we pray what God desires, we can
pray with confidence that God will answer
our prayer!

And we can be assured that those who
walk in wisdom make right choices. Those
who seek to walk worthy of the Lord keep
God's commandments and are in position,
therefore, to receive the fullness of God's
blessings. Those who have a greater and
greater knowledge of the Lord are increasingly sensitive to His voice of warning,
caution, comfort, and counsel.

The stronger we are in the Lord, the
greater we will display His character to the
world. The more thankful we are, the more
we will have a zest for living and an awareness of God's goodness toward us. The
more mindful we are of the power we have
been given over the enemy, the stronger
the stance we will take in confronting evil
and resisting temptation.

Oh, the life God desires for us! Learn
this prayer. Pray it often for yourself and
your family members.

Teach Your Children to Pray Bible-Based Prayers

Teach your children to pray this prayer in Colossians 1:9–14 for themselves. Teach your children by your example and by daily training to give thanks to God for everything good that happens to them, to praise God for who He is in their lives and for what He has done on their behalf, and to ask God for the things they need. Teach your children to trust God in all things — to openly profess their relationship with Him and to be bold in their testimony about who God is and what God desires to do on this earth.

Teach your children to pray for understanding as they read the Word of God. The devil's objective is to draw your children away from God, to thwart His purposes for their lives at the earliest age possible, to get them to deny God, and ultimately to destroy them. If you don't instruct your children about the devil's strategies and the ways in which they are to respond to temptation, who will? The society as a whole certainly won't! I don't know too many adults today who, if they were teenagers today, would be able to withstand the onslaught of messages that are filled with sexual passion, sensuality, immorality, violence, compromise, corruption, and lack of truth. You must teach and train your children with the truth.

Let your children hear you praying aloud for them. Don't send your children out into a society and a general educational system without praying for and with them. A child is never immune from the temptations of the devil.

Your children are confronted with sex, drugs, bullets, and bombs. The world into which they go every morning is marked by evil, including molesters and kidnappers and drug dealers. You haven't prepared your children for school unless you have reminded them about God's protection, God's love, and God's presence with them. Send your children to school with a hug and a prayer.

Encourage your children to memorize God's Word and to incorporate Bible verses into their prayers and into the way they speak to themselves to encourage themselves, and to feel confident in times when they are unsure of what to say or do, when they are fearful, or when they face a difficult situation.

A Story of Victory

At the beginning of this chapter I mentioned to you a father who came to me desperately desiring for his family to be restored and reconciled. I encouraged and admonished this man to do the following:

- Confess his sin to the Lord and receive God's forgiveness. He did.
- Read God's Word faithfully to more fully understand his position in Christ Jesus. He did.
- Begin to do the right things — to get help for his addiction, to help his wife seek out help for her addiction, to attend church regularly, to begin to lift up the name of Jesus in his home, and to cleanse his home of anything that was not in accordance with God's commands. He did.
- Pray diligently and at length for his wife and children. He did.

This man did what he knew was God's plan for protecting his family. And God did what no human being can do.

He healed this man and each of his family members in profound ways.

He renewed their love for one another.

He restored their souls, and He made them strong in their faith.

What God did in their lives continues today, nearly twenty years later. What God did for him, He can and will do for you — as individuals and as a family. God does not want to see you fall victim to the devil. He will move heaven and earth to help you resist the devil's temptations, quench the fiery darts of the devil, and stand strong in Christ Jesus. Trust God to help you today.

Conclusion

The enemy *will* strike. It's not a matter of *if;* it's a matter of *when*. And when he does, God takes action — not in equal measure, but in greater strength and in greater authority. Our role is to open ourselves to receiving all of God's power at work on our behalf. Our role is to recognize that when bad things happen in our lives, there is a force behind the evil deeds of men and women. Satan's desire is to steal from you, to destroy you, and ultimately to separate you from God's purposes and God's presence.

God's desire is *always* for you to experience a full and satisfying life on this earth and eternal life with Him in heaven. Put yourself squarely on God's side, which is always the winning side. Ask God to help you identify the enemy's tricks. Trust Him to do it!

Ask the Lord to free you from any snares that have entangled you. Ask Him to free you from the things that continually infuse debate into your conversations, division in your relationships, doubt into your faith, or deception into your thinking. Speak the truth of God to your heart and mind.

When the enemy strikes, ask the Lord to help you discern as fully as possible the true nature of the situation. Ask the Lord to help you to see and understand as He sees and understands, and then to make godly judgments and right choices. Ask Him to make very clear to you what is good and what is evil, what is real and what is illusion, what is good and what is best, and what you desire that may be contrary to what God may have planned. Make a choice to live out God's will, to obey God's commands, and to activate your faith as you exercise godly judgment.

When the enemy sends fiery darts of fear, guilt, lust, anger, pride, and other ungodly thoughts into your mind, refuse to allow those thoughts to lodge in you. Don't dwell on them or fantasize about them. Don't allow them to become a toehold, a foothold, or a stronghold in your life. Seize the critical moment of decision to turn your thinking toward what is godly — be quick to say no to any temptation to contemplate evil or act on it. Choose to take every thought captive to Christ Jesus and, in so doing, to resist the temptations of the devil.

When the enemy strikes, take a look at your level of neediness. Ask yourself, *Why am I vulnerable to this temptation? What need am I failing to trust God to meet?* Pause to think about the end consequences if you act on a particular temptation. Refuse to use the typical excuses and self-justifications for sinning. Don't play the blame game. Learn how to resist the devil and to build safeguards into your life to help you withstand the devil's temptations.

Distance yourself from the devil at every opportunity!

Learn and use God's Word in resisting Satan — just as Jesus did.

At all times, stay dressed for battle, fully clothing yourself in the identity of Christ so that

- your relationships and decisions are based upon and function according to God's truth.
- your emotions and spontaneous choices are marked by righteousness — they flow almost instinctively from your right relationship with Christ Jesus.

- your attitudes and desires are for God's peace to prevail in all situations and in all relationships.

Keep yourself well armed with

- bold and great faith — trusting in a mighty God and believing as you stand with other believers for nothing less than God's best.
- an awareness of your salvation and of God's desire to save others.
- a fresh remembrance of God's Word, knowing at all times that God's Word is unchanging and totally applicable to every situation you face.

Put on the whole armor of God daily, which is having a fresh awareness and a renewed acceptance by faith of this powerful truth: you in Christ and Christ in you!

Pray and intercede in the Spirit. Praise and give thanks to God. Place your petitions before Him. Live in an atmosphere of prayer at all times, being quick to talk to God about every aspect of every day. Watch and persevere in your prayers.

Stand strong and steadfast as you anticipate God's help. Trust Him to work in you, through you, and around you to bring about His ultimate plans and eternal purposes.

The Lord has provided for you all that you need to overcome every attack of the enemy. Receive what He has provided. Act on it. You *will* have all you need to be victorious even against the fiercest assault of the enemy.

About the Author

Dr. Charles F. Stanley is pastor of the 15,000-member First Baptist Church in Atlanta, Georgia, and is president and CEO of IN TOUCH Ministries. He has twice been elected president of the Southern Baptist Convention and is well-known internationally through his IN TOUCH radio and television ministry. His many best-selling books include *Finding Peace, Walking Wisely, When Tragedy Strikes, Charles Stanley's Handbook for Christian Living, A Touch of His Power, Our Unmet Needs, Enter His Gates,* and *The Source of My Strength.*